THE JEWISH AMERICANS

A HISTORY IN THEIR OWN WORDS 1650–1950

THE JEWISH AMERICANS

A HISTORY
IN THEIR
OWN WORDS
1650–1950

EDITED BY
MILTON MELTZER

THOMAS Y. CROWELL   NEW YORK

Library of Congress Cataloging in Publication Data
Meltzer, Milton, 1915–
    The Jewish Americans.
    Bibliography: p.   Includes index.
    Summary: A collection of accounts of personal experiences
of Jewish Americans, taken from letters, journals, diaries,
autobiographies, speeches, and other documents.
    1. Jews—United States—History—Juvenile literature.
2. United States—Ethnic relations—Juvenile literature.
[1. Jews—United States—History—Sources.   2. United
States—Ethnic relations]   I. Title.
E184.J5M448 1982   973'.04924   81–43886
ISBN 0–690–04227–2   AACR2
ISBN 0–690–04228–0 (lib. bdg.)

1 2 3 4 5 6 7 8 9 10

First Edition

Contents

Preface

In this book I try to give the past a place in what we think and feel now. I write as a Jewish American sharing in a collective memory. For some of us that past is unknown, dim, or forgotten. We may try to grasp it by reading history. But history, whether of Jews or of any other people, is often painfully dry. It deals with leaders—with statesmen, generals, or politicians; it deals with laws and economics, with sweeping movements and catchphrase epochs. Where are the people who made that history—the anonymous people whose names are not in the Hall of Fame?

Some of them are in this book. The ancestors of today's Jewish Americans tell about their own lives, in their own words. What they say to us is not a substitute for history. It is only a part of it, but one sorely neglected. Their voices speak of personal experience, so that we come to feel what it was like to be alive in their time and their place. These ancestors of today's Jewish Americans enrich our group memory and help us recover from the past what still lives.

To use a scholarly term, we could call this book a documentary history, but not in the usual sense of official papers—constitutions, laws, treaties, judicial decisions. Important as those are, they are rarely readable and never personal. Here we have another kind of document—the voices of people taken from their letters, journals, diaries, autobiographies, speeches, petitions, and interviews. They reveal to us their joys, fears, expectations, griefs, protests, achievements.

Each voice is introduced by a note identifying the speaker and the event or experience he or she describes. Some of the documents are given in full; many have been shortened, but in such a way that their meaning is not changed. In some cases I have taken the liberty of paragraphing and of modernizing spelling and punctuation for easier reading. At the end of each document, I cite its source. The index will help the reader trace people, events, and topics.

This volume begins with life in the earliest years of colonial America, when the first handful of Jews arrived. It ends in 1950, shortly after the Second World War, when some survivors of the Holocaust began their migration to a very different America.

Introduction

On a September day in 1654, the SAINT CHARLES *sailed into the port of New Amsterdam and left twenty-three penniless passengers on the wharf. They were Jews fleeing from persecution by the Portuguese in Brazil. The governor of New Amsterdam, Peter Stuyvesant, did not wish to let "such hateful enemies of Christ" stay. But his masters in Holland ordered him to admit the new colonists.*

Those twenty-three refugees formed the first permanent community of Jews in what is now the United States. They settled here scarcely thirty years after the Puritans came to Massachusetts. But the history of Jewish Americans begins much earlier. It is linked to the "discovery" of the New World and to the conditions in Europe that led the Jews to migrate to the Americas.

The passengers debarking from the SAINT CHARLES were Sephardic Jews—Jews who stemmed from the Iberian peninsula. There, in Spain and Portugal, Jews had known a golden age for several centuries. Encouraged by the enlightened Mohammedans who ruled southern Spain, the Jews developed their own communal life and shared in the nurture of every brand of the arts and sciences. Long as that happier time lasted, it was but one chapter in the 4,000-year history of the Jews. The Roman conquest of their homeland in Palestine in the first century CE (Christian Era) had dispersed the Jews to the far corners of the earth. Though torn from their Temple in Jerusalem, the Jews kept their faith. In the Diaspora the scattered communities of Jews learned to rely on themselves to maintain the sacred teachings and the laws of Judaism.

Throughout the Middle Ages in Europe the Jews were only a tolerated people. The established religion of Christianity used its power to make Jews outcasts when they would not convert. It permitted them no citizenship or rights. They were shut out from the honorable ways of making a living. Farming and owning land were banned. The craft guilds excluded them. Because Christians were not supposed to enter trade, commerce became the only occupation left to Jews. Then, as Europe's economy developed, trade attracted Christians, and Jews were displaced. They turned to banking and finance. Soon Christians began to replace Jewish financiers also while the merchant guilds shut their doors to Jewish traders.

In those centuries of uncertainty, Jews wandered from place to place, their roots torn up, their survival menaced, their hopes blighted. Still, they managed to play a great role in the exchange of ideas as well as of commercial products. Culture in the medieval world owed much to Jewish learning. As physicians, inventors, financiers, philosophers, translators, Jews served the princes of state and church. They were a force in awakening Europe to a new intellectual life.

When the militant church launched the Crusades in 1095, it was a disaster for the Jews. On their way to crush the infidels in the Holy Land, the Crusaders paused again and again to slaughter Jewish unbelievers. A church council in 1215 ordered Jews to wear a yellow badge on their clothing and drove them into a segregated life behind ghetto walls. As anti-Jewish feeling mounted, its victims were robbed, tortured, exiled, massacred.

Their martyrdom led to another great wave of migration. From Germany and central Europe, Jews fled to Poland where their skills and energy were welcomed for a time. The Moslems in Spain also welcomed Jews. But when Moorish power was broken, the position of the Jews crumbled. Under the Inquisition, Spain conducted a reign of terror against the Jews. Finally, they were ordered out of Spain. Allowed to take nothing with them, they scattered in all directions.

Where could they find a haven—a place where they could use their talents, their experience, their enterprise? On the day following their forced departure from Spain in 1492, Christopher Columbus set sail on the voyage that would ultimately provide that haven. (Jews played a part in making his expedition to the New World a success. Their discoveries in mathematics, in geography, mapmaking, and navigation proved of great value to pioneers of the sea.)

But Jews expelled from Spain knew better than to seek homes at once in New World colonies. They settled first in Holland and elsewhere until the terror of the Inquisition diminished. Some took refuge in Brazil when the more tolerant Dutch controlled it. After the Portuguese ousted the Dutch, the first small band of Jews fled to New Amsterdam.

THE JEWISH AMERICANS

A HISTORY
IN THEIR
OWN WORDS
1650-1950

Do Not Shut Us Out

The two dozen Jews settled down in New Amsterdam. But Peter Stuyvesant did not make life easy for them. They were barred from owning land, trading with the Indians, entering crafts, or holding public office. Nor could they practice their religion in a synagogue or public gathering.

For America was not yet a free land. The settlers carried with them from the Old World many of their religious prejudices. Jews were a tiny minority among other religious minorities. Many of the early settlers came in search of greater religious freedom for themselves. But they were not ready to give others the same freedom. The Puritans, for instance, sometimes flogged Catholics and once hung four Quakers on Boston Common. Both Roger Williams and Anne Hutchinson were driven from Massachusetts Bay colony because they were religious dissenters.

The Jews in New Amsterdam wanted to share guard duty. The authorities refused them and imposed a special tax in place of military service. Young Asser Levy, a butcher by trade, fought the discrimination and was finally allowed to serve. Then he demanded his full rights as a burgher and freeman. When the court rejected his plea in 1657, the Jews of the colony sent this successful appeal to the authorities.

To the Noble Worships, the Director General and Council of New Netherland:

We, the undersigned of the Jewish nation here, make known, with due reverence, how that one of our nation [Asser Levy] repaired to the City Hall of this city and requested of the Noble Burgomasters that he might obtain his burgher certificate, like other burghers, which to our great surprise was declined and refused by the Noble Burgomasters, and,

Whereas the Worshipful Lords [in Amsterdam] consented under date of February 15, 1655, at the request of our nation,

1

that we should enjoy here the same freedom as other inhabitants of New Netherland enjoy, as appears from the petition here annexed;

Further, that our nation enjoys in the city of Amsterdam in Holland the burgher right, and he who asks therefore receives a burgher certificate there, as appears by the burgher certificate hereto annexed; also that our nation, as long as they have been here, with others, borne and paid, and still bear, all burgher burdens;

We, therefore, reverently request your Noble Worships to please not exclude nor shut us out from the burgher right, but to notify the Noble Burgomasters that they should permit us, like other burghers, to enjoy the burgher right, and for this purpose to give us the customary burgher certificate, in conformity with the order of the Worshipful Lords Directors above mentioned. Upon which, awaiting your Noble Worships' gracious and favorable apostille [endorsement], we shall remain, as heretofore,

Your Noble Worships' humble servants,
Salvador Dandrada, Jacob Cohen Henricques, Abraham
DeLucena, Joseph d'Acosta.

Publications of the American Jewish Historical Society, XVIII, 1909

Why Should the Pickles Be Spoilt?

Few though the Jews were, they played a useful part in the commercial and social life of the colonies. Jewish merchants carried on trade between

*the colonies and abroad, and in time, with the Indians. Some helped
open up the West, dealing in lands and trading furs. Others entered
crafts, as barriers to those occupations came down. Jews were bakers,
tailors, silversmiths, peruke makers.*

*In young America there were no ghettos. Jews lived side by side
with the Gentiles. The Franks family was typical of Jews who prospered
in the New World. Jacob Franks had came from England to serve the
British as a business agent in the colonies. He became one of New
York's wealthiest Jews. In his elegant mansion he enjoyed an aristocratic
life. He sent his young son Naphtali, called Heartsey, to England to
be educated. Naphtali's mother, Abigail, wrote her first son frequently,
sending him both news and advice.*

Dear Heartsey:

I have three of your letters answered. The first of them
brought us the melancholy account of the death of that
worthy and good man Mr. Isaac Franks [your father's
brother, d. 1736] which truly was a very great shock, especially to your father, who for a long while had been very
uneasy on account of his brother's indisposition. . . . Your
father seemed immovable for some time. At last he broke
out in a flood of tears. He was very melancholy for a long
time, but now begins to be more settled.

For my part when I find a person has so great a cause
for grief I can say but little by way of relief, knowing nature
has its call upon these occasions and nothing but time and
reason to assuage the dolor. . . . He was but a very young
man, "but in the grave there is no inquisition whether a
man be ten, twenty, or a hundred years old." All the difference after death is a man's works here on earth, for that
never dies, and one that has left so great and good a name
may be said to have lived full of days and died in a good
old age. . . .

I am sensibly concerned at what happened in your Uncle

Jacob Franks, who came from England to serve the British as a business agent in the colonies, became one of New York's wealthiest Jews.

Abraham [Franks's] family with regard to his daughter. But it's what I always expected, for they will not consent [by providing liberal dowries] to let them have husbands because the Jews with best fortunes will not have them, so they can't blame them if they choose for themselves. I am really concerned for your uncle and wish him better luck with his other daughters. . . . Pray give my humble service to him and family. . . .

I can't tell what should be the reason the pickles should be spoilt, unless the vinegar runs off while they are onboard ship, or else they are too long in the cold and so freeze. For I keep of the very same for my own use and they always keep good until the return of the season, except this year, and then it was a general calamity, for the weather was so cold that everything froze and so of consequence spoilt. However I shall send you some again this year which hope may prove better. The silks you sent are very dear, but give my service to Sam Levy and tell him the tea was very good.

I shall be very glad . . . that you would send us some little amusements which you have been very remiss of of late. . . . Pray send me the 2d vol. of the *Revolution of Poland,* the first you sent some time ago; also 2 bottles of the best Scotch snuff for my own use and 2 pr. spectacles of the very best.

I have endeavored by a sort of medley to make a long letter for which I'll make no excuse, but would have you take it as a testimony of the pleasure I take in saying something to you, and let this assure you that I am, dear child,

Your most affectionate mother,
Abigail Franks

New York, June the 5th, 1737

Jacob R. Marcus, *Early American Jewry,* Vol. I (Philadelphia, Jewish Publication Society, 1951)

A Single, Modest, Sober Person

Some time after the British took over New Amsterdam and renamed it New York, they let the Jews form congregations and build synagogues. Under the Dutch, the Jews, like the Lutherans and Catholics, could hold services only privately, in their own homes. In 1730 the Sephardic Jews built the first synagogue in America, Shearith Israel, which means the Remnant of Israel. Its site was downtown in the Wall Street district. Today the congregation, the oldest in the country, occupies a synagogue on Central Park West.

The Sephardic Jews were not like the Jews of the rest of Europe, who in 1215 had been forced by the church to live apart from Christians, behind the walls of ghettos. They had known no ghettos in Spain or Portugal in the centuries before their expulsion. They were not orthodox in the traditional ways. Most of them wore the same clothes as the Christians. Each congregation was independent. Its members were responsible to no higher Judaic authority, but only to themselves and the public law.

In this letter, the elders of Shearith Israel request that a teacher be hired to instruct their children in the Hebrew tongue. His qualifications and duties are spelled out carefully.

December 16, 1760

Mr. Benj. Pereira
Sir:

After our compliments to you and your family we take this opportunity to acquaint you that at a meeting of the elders . . . it was agreed that we should apply to you and that you will be good enough to engage a suitable master capable to teach our children the Hebrew language. English and Spanish he ought to know, but he will not suit unless he understands Hebrew and English at least. This must require your particular care: a single, modest, sober person will be most agreeable. However, on your good judgement we shall depend, as you very well know our minds and tempers and can make choice of such as will be suitable and capable of the undertaking. He must oblige himself to keep a public school at the usual hours of the forenoons on every customary day of your Yeshiva.

Children whose parents are in needy circumstances he must teach gratis. His salary shall be first at forty pounds New York money per year and shall commence from the day of his arrival here. And all other children he teaches must and will pay him as has been done heretofore. We flatter ourselves you will excuse the trouble we give you as it will very much oblige our whole congregation and in a more particular manner the Parnassim who are

Sir your most ob't humble servants

Jacob R. Marcus, *Sourcebook for American Jewish History*

The first prayer book for Jewish holidays to be published in the American colonies appeared in New York in 1761. AMERICAN JEWISH HISTORICAL SOCIETY

Evening Service

 O F *Levy*

ROSHASHANAH,

AND

KIPPUR.

O R

The BEGINNING of the YEAR,

AND

The DAY of ATONEMENT.

NEW-YORK:
Printed by *W. Weyman*, in *Broad-Street*, MDCCLXI.

Merchantable Young Slaves

*In Newport, Rhode Island, Jewish merchants were very active in the
sea trade. Aaron Lopez owned a fleet of some thirty vessels and shipped
cargoes of everything from horses to lumber to soap to the West Indies,
England, and Africa. From England he imported cotton, hoes, and guns;
from the West Indies, molasses for rum; and from Africa, slaves.*

*Slaves were central to the triangular trade, and Newport was the
major colonial port for traffic in human beings. The "best" people took
part in it, including the most prestigious families of New England,
who drew their wealth largely from slavery. Only a handful of whites
questioned its morality in the first 200 years of American slavery.*

*Isaac Elizer and Samuel Moses, two of the town's Jewish merchants,
took part in the slave trade. In this letter they give the captain of one
of their ships his sailing orders for Africa.*

Newport, Octo'r 29, 1762

Captain John Peck:

As you are at present master of the sloop *Prince George* with
her cargo on board and ready to sail, you are to observe
the following orders:

That you embrace the first fair wind and proceed to sea
and make the best of your way to the windward part of
the coast of Africa, and at your arrival there dispose of
your cargo for the most possible can be gotten, and invest
the net proceeds into as many good merchantable young
slaves as you can, and make all the dispatch you possibly
can.

As soon as your business there is completed, make the
best of your way from thence to the island of New Provi-

dence [Bahamas] and there dispose of your slaves for cash, if the markets are not too dull. But if they should be, make the best of your way home to this port, take pilots and make proper protest [before the authorities as to the state of your cargo or vessel] wherever you find it necessary. You are further to observe that all the rum on board your sloop shall come upon an average in case of any misfortune and also all the slaves in general shall come upon an average in case any casualty or misfortune happens, and that no slaves shall be brought upon freight for any person, neither direct nor indirect.

And also we allow you for your commission, four slaves upon the purchase of one hundred and four, and the privilege of bringing home three slaves, and your mate, one.

Observe not neglect writing us by all opportunities of every transaction of your voyage. Lastly be particular careful of your vessel and slaves, and be as frugal as possible in every expense relating to the voyage. So wish you a good voyage, and are your owners and humble servants.

But further observe, if you dispose of your slaves in Providence [Bahamas], lay out as much of your net proceeds as will load your vessel in any commodity of that island, that will be best for our advantage, and the remainder of your effects bring home in money.

Isaac Elizer,
Samuel Moses.

Massachusetts Historical Society Collections, 7 Ser., IX

The First to Die

On the eve of the American Revolution, no more than 2,500 Jews lived in the colonies. They represented less than one-tenth of one percent of the total population. When the fighting began, most of the Jews served the cause of freedom. Jewish merchants and tradesmen, especially, were among the first colonials to suffer from Britain's restrictive measures. Some Jews, like many Christians, remained loyal to the king.

Only a small number of the Jews were young enough to bear arms for the new republic. About 100 fought, many of them winning honor and distinction. Among them was Francis Salvador, who had migrated from England to South Carolina in 1773, where he soon acquired a 7,000-acre plantation and many slaves. Still in his twenties, he joined the resistance to British rule and was elected to the provincial congress. He thus became the first American Jew to hold state office.

Salvador joined Major Andrew Williamson's regiment to fight against the British, the Tories, and their Indian allies, who had grievances against the colonials. In this letter Salvador writes to Chief Justice William A. Drayton, reporting the action in his district.

Two weeks later, his regiment was ambushed. Salvador was shot three times and scalped while still alive. He died within an hour. He was probably the first Jew to give his life in defense of the new nation.

Camp near Dewett's Corner, 18th July, 1776

Dear Sir:

. . . You would have been surprised to have seen the change in this country two days after you left me. On Monday morning one of Capt. Smith's sons came to my house with two of his fingers shot off and gave an account of the shocking catastrophe at his father's. [The Indians had killed his parents and two of his brothers and sisters.]

I immediately galloped to Major Williamson's to inform him but found another of Smith's sons there, who had made his escape and alarmed that settlement. The whole country was flying—some to make forts, others as low as Orangeburgh.

Williamson was employed night and day sending expresses to raise the militia, but the panic was so great that the Wednesday following, the Major and myself marched to the late Capt. Smith's with only forty men. The next day we were joined by forty more and have been gradually increasing ever since, tho' all the men in the country were loath to turn out till they have procured some kind of fancied security for their families. However, we had last night 500 men, but have not been joined by any from the other side of the [Saluda] River. I rode there last Saturday and found Col. Williams and Lisles and two companies from Col. Richardson's regiment, amounting to 430 men.

They were attacked on Monday morning, July 15th, by Indians and Scopholites [Tories and partisans], but repulsed them, taking thirteen white men prisoners. The Indians fled the moment day appeared. . . .

I am afraid the burden of the war will fall on this regiment, and that the people over the river will do nothing. They grumble at being commanded by a Major; and, I fear, if they join us at all, which I doubt, they will be very apt to prejudice the service by altercations about command. . . .

Our men seem spirited and very much exasperated against our enemies. They are all displeased with the people over the River for granting quarter to their prisoners, and declare they will grant none either to Indians or white men who join them. We have just received an account that two of the Cherokees' head warriors were killed in the late skirmish at Lindley's Fort, 19th July.

. . . We have just heard from over the River that the white people in general [the Tories] had quitted the Indians after the repulse at Lindley's and were delivering themselves up to Col. Lisles. He has sent all these to Ninety-Six jail against whom there is proof of having been in the action.

I hope you will pardon the freedom with which I express

my sentiments, but I look upon it as an advantage to men in power to be truly informed of the people's situation and disposition. This must plead my excuse, and believe me to be, with great respect, dear sir,

Your most obedient humble servant,
Francis Salvador

P.S. We, this day, increased to 600, all from the same regiment. Capt. [James] McCall, with twenty men, was sent by Major Williamson to the Cherokees at Seneca to make prisoners of some white men [Tories], by the encouragement of some Indians who had been at the Major's. When the detachment got near, the Indians came out to meet them, spoke friendly to them, and invited the captain, lieutenant, and another man to sup with them, leaving three of their own people in their room. And, in a few hours after, in the night, the Indians returned and suddenly attacked the detachment which fled as fast as possible. They are all returned but the captain and six men.

This happened immediately before Smith's family was cut off, who lost five Negro men, himself, wife and five children.

John Drayton, *Memoirs of the American Revolution,* 1821

This House Swarmed with Beaux

In the first year of the revolutionary war, New York City was captured and occupied by British troops. Many wealthy colonials had taken the side of the British and were pleased. One such Tory was David Franks, a Jewish merchant from Philadelphia. He was partner to Jews and to non-Jews in many business ventures. In 1781 one of his daughters, Rebecca, was spending the summer at the country estate of the Van Horns in Flatbush, Brooklyn. She writes her sister Abigail a long, chatty letter. It shows that even in the midst of war, society managed to entertain itself. After the war, the victorious Americans imprisoned David Franks for a time and took away all his property.

Flatbush, Saturday, 10 o'clock, August 10, 1781

My dear Abby:

. . . You ask a description of the Miss Van Horn that was with me, Cornelia. She is in disposition as fine a girl as ever you saw, a great deal of good humor and good sense. Her person is too large for a beauty, in my opinion (and yet I am not partial to a little woman). Her complexion, eyes, and teeth are very good, and a great quantity of light brown hair (Entre nous, the girls of New York excel us Philadelphians in that particular and in their form), a sweet countenance and agreeable smile. Her feet, as you desire, I'll say nothing about. . . . But her sister Kitty is the belle of the family, I think, though some give the preference to Betsy. . . .

By the by, few New York ladies know how to entertain company in their own houses unless they introduce the card tables, except this family (who are remarkable for their good sense and ease). I don't know a woman or girl that can chat above half an hour, and that's on the form of a cap, the color of a ribbon, or the set of a hoop stay or jupon [petticoat]. I will do our ladies, that is Philadelphians, the justice to say they have more cleverness in the turn of an eye than the New York girls have in their whole composition. With what ease, have I seen a Chew, a Penn, Oswald, Allen, and a thousand others entertain a large circle

13

of both sexes, and the conversation without the aid of cards not flag or seem the least strained or stupid.

Here, or more properly speaking in New York, you enter the room with a formal set curtsy and after the how do's, 'tis a fine or a bad day, and those trifling nothings are finished, then all's a dead calm 'till the cards are introduced when you see pleasure dancing in the eyes of all the matrons, and they seem to gain new life. The misses, if they have a favorite swain, frequently decline playing for the pleasure of making love, for to all appearances 'tis the ladies and not the gentlemen that show a preference nowadays. 'Tis here, I fancy, always leap year. For my part that am used to quite another mode of behavior, cannot help showing my surprise, perhaps they call it ignorance, when I see a lady single out her pet to lean almost in his arms at an assembly or play house (which I give my honor I have too often seen both in married and single), and to hear a lady confess a partiality for a man who perhaps she has not seen three times. [She might say,] "Well, I declare, such a gentleman is a delightful creature and I could love him for my husband," or "I could marry such or such a person." And scandal says [with respect to] most who have been married, the advances have first come from the ladies' side. Or she has got a male friend to introduce him and puff her off. 'Tis really the case, and with me they lose half their charms; and I fancy there would be more marriage was another mode adopted. But they've made the men so saucy that I sincerely believe the lowest ensign thinks 'tis but ask and have; a red coat and smart epaulet is sufficient to secure a female heart. . . .

Well, this is sufficiently long; love to everybody. . .

Yours,

R. F.

Manuscript, Historical Society of Pennsylvania

Rich I Am Not

*Haym Solomon emigrated to America from Poland in about the year
1764, when he was in his mid-twenties. According to a widespread
myth he helped to finance the Revolution with huge sums of money.
Solomon himself never made such a claim. And research has proved
there is no truth to it. He did help the American cause by selling
government war bonds, and he lent money to such revolutionary leaders
as James Madison and Edmund Randolph, often charging no interest.*

*Early in the war, Solomon fled New York to avoid capture by the
British and made Philadelphia his base of operations. Relatives abroad,
hearing he was rich, sought his help again and again. In this letter,
he replies to an uncle living in England.*

Philadelphia, 10 July, 1783

Dear Uncle:

. . . I have ordered fifty guilders to be paid you by Mr.
Gumple Samson in Amsterdam, which letter giving that
order you must already have received, and I now send you
an order for six guineas.

Your bias of my riches is too extensive. Rich I am not,
but the little I have I think it my duty to share with my
poor father and mother. They are the first that are to be
provided for by me, and must and shall have the preference.
Whatever little more I can squeeze out I will give my relations, but I tell you plainly and truly that it is not in my
power to give you or any relations yearly allowances. Don't
you nor any of them expect it. Don't fill your mind with
vain and idle expectations and golden dreams that never
will nor can be accomplished. Besides my father and mother,
my wife and children must be provided for. I have three
young children, and as my wife is very young may have

more, and if you and the rest of my relations will consider things with reason, they will be sensible of this I now write. But notwithstanding this I mean to assist my relations as far as lays in my power.

I am much surprised at your intention of coming here. Your *yikes* is worth very little here: nor can I imagine what you mean to do here. I think your duty calls for your going to your family, and besides these six guineas you will receive in Amsterdam fifty guineas of Mr. Gumple Samson.

You are pleased to say you have done a great deal for my family. Let my father and the *a'bd dk'k Lissa* ["rabbi of Lissa"] write me the particular services you have done to my family, and I will consider in what manner to recompense them.

I desire no relation may be sent. Have I not children, are they not relations? When I shall be fully informed of all the young people of our family and their qualifications explained, I may then perhaps advise sending one or two to this country, and I will at my leisure explain to you the nature of this country: *vinig yidishkayt.*

> I am, with true respect, dear uncle,
> Your affectionate nephew,
> Your very humble servant
> Haym Salomon

Jacob R. Marcus, *Early American Jewry*, Vol I

For Freedom of Religion

After the triumph of the revolutionary cause, the new American nation struggled to devise a system of law and government to live by. In 1787 delegates from the thirteen states met in Philadelphia to write a constitution. The relationship it established between religion and government was of special concern to Jews and all other religious minorities. If church and state were linked, would not a citizen's inherent freedom to worship as he pleased be endangered?

Separation of church and state was not a new concept. It had been introduced over a hundred years earlier by Roger Williams and William Penn. A year before the constitutional convention met, Thomas Jefferson's bill to establish religious freedom had been adopted as law in Virginia.

In 1787 Jonas Phillips sent the following letter to the Constitutional Convention, petitioning it to guarantee religious freedom and explaining why such freedom was needed. Phillips, a German-born Jew who had migrated to America in 1756 at the age of twenty, was president of his Philadelphia congregation.

The convention did vote to include a clause in Article Six of the Constitution stating that no religious test should be required of officeholders. But many people did not consider this to be far-reaching enough. In 1789 Congress adopted the ten amendments to the Constitution known as the Bill of Rights. The First Amendment states: "Congress shall make no law respecting the establishment of religion, or prohibiting the free exercise thereof . . ."

That amendment would have a profound effect upon American Jews and of course on people of all faiths. Under the Constitution, each citizen was now free to practice any religion he or she chose. The path was open for people of any religion or of no religion to hold office in any branch of government.

September 7, 1787

Sirs:

With leave and submission I address myself to those in whom there is wisdom, understanding, and knowledge; they are the honorable personages appointed and made overseers

17

of a part of the terrestrial globe of the earth, namely the 13 United States of America in Convention Assembled. The Lord preserve them, amen—

I the subscriber being one of the people called Jews, of the City of Philadelphia, a people scattered and dispersed among all nations, do behold with concern that among the laws in the Constitution of Pennsylvania, there is a clause Sect. 10, to viz—"I do believe in one God, the Creature [sic] and governor of the universe, the rewarder of the good and the punisher of the wicked—and I do acknowledge the Scriptures of the Old and New Testament to be given by divine inspiration."

To swear and believe that the New Testament was given by divine inspiration is absolutely against the religious principle of a Jew, and is against his conscience to take any such oath. By the above law a Jew is deprived of holding any public office or place of government, which is contradictory to the Bill of Rights, Sec. 2 viz:

"That all men have a natural and unalienable right to worship almighty God according to the dictates of their own conscience and understanding, and that no man ought or of right can be compelled to attend any religious worship or creed or support any place of worship or maintain any minister contrary to or against his own free will and consent, nor can any man who acknowledges the being of a God be justly deprived or abridged of any civil right as a citizen on account of his religious sentiments or peculiar mode of religious worship, and that no authority can or ought to be vested in or assumed by any power whatever that shall in any case interfere or in any manner control the right of conscience in the free exercise of religious worship."

It is well-known among all the citizens of the 13 United States that the Jews have been true and faithful Whigs, and during the late contest with England they have been foremost in aiding and assisting the states with their lifes

18

and fortunes. They have supported the cause, have bravely fought and bled for liberty which they cannot enjoy.

Therefore, if the honorable convention shall in their wisdom think fit, and alter the said oath, and leave out the words, to viz: "and I do acknowledge the scripture of the New Testament to be given by divine inspiration," then the Israelites will think themself happy to live under a government where all religious societies are on an equal footing. I solicit this favor for myself, my children and posterity, and for the benefit of all the Israelites through the 13 United States of America. . . .

Your most devoted obedient servant
Jonas Phillips

American Jewish Historical Society Proceedings, II, 1894

To Bigotry No Sanction

After George Washington's inauguration in 1789, several Jewish congregations sent greetings to the new president. Among these messages was one from the Jews of Newport, Rhode Island. It welcomed the president on his visit to the city and stated how much it meant to Jews to live under a government that "gives to bigotry no sanction, to persecution no assistance." Washington replied warmly to each such address. He said American citizens had the right to applaud themselves for setting for the world the example of freedom.

To the President of the United States of America
Sir:

Permit the children of the stock of Abraham to approach

you with the most cordial affection and esteem for your person and merits, and to join with our fellow citizens in welcoming you to Newport.

With pleasure we reflect on those days, those days of difficulty and danger, when the God of Israel, who delivered David from the peril of the sword—shielded your head in the day of battle—and we rejoice to think that the same spirit who rested in the bosom of the greatly beloved Daniel, enabling him to preside over the provinces of the Babylon-

This Rhode Island newspaper carried on page one the address from the Hebrew Congregation of Newport to George Washington when he visited Providence on August 17, 1790. On the right is the president's reply.

The Providence Gazette and Country Journ

(N° 38, of Vol. XXVII.)   SATURDAY, *September* 18; 1790.   (N° 13

Publiſhed by *JOHN CARTER*, at the Poſt-Office, near the State-Houſe.

The following ADDRESSES *were preſented to the* PRESIDENT *of the* UNITED STATES, *at* NEWPORT.

ADDRESS *from the* CITIZENS *of* NEWPORT. *To the* PRESIDENT *of the* UNITED STATES *of* AMERICA.

SIR,

IMPRESSED with the livelieſt ſentiments of gratitude and affeÉtion, the citizens of Newport ſalute you on your arrival in this State, and wiſh to expreſs their joy on this intereſting occaſion.

The preſent circumſtances of this town forbid ſome of thoſe demonſtrations of gratitude and reſpeÉt, which the citizens of our ſiſter States have diſplayed on a ſimilar occaſion; yet we rejoice in this opportunity of tendering the richeſt offering which a free people can make —hearts ſincerely devoted to you, and to the government over which you preſide.

We anticipate with pleaſing expeÉtation the happy period, when, under the auſpicious government of the united States, our languiſhing commerce ſhall revive, and our loſſes be repaired—when commerce at large expand her wings in every quarter of the globe, and arts, manufaÉtures and agriculture, be carried to the higheſt pitch of improvement.

May kind Providence long continue your invaluable life; and in the progreſſive advancement of the United States in opulence, order and felicity, may you realize the moſt glorious proſpeÉt which humanity can exhibit —an enlightened and benevolent legiſlator; and when you ſhall ceaſe to be mortal, may you be aſſociated to the moſt perfeÉt ſociety in the realms above, and receive the retribution for your diſintereſted and extenſive ſervices, which the JUDGE of all the earth will beſtow on the friends of piety, virtue and mankind.

By Order,
H. MARCHANT, Moderator.

The ANSWER.
To the FREEMEN *of the Town of* NEWPORT.

GENTLEMEN,

I RECEIVE with emotions of ſatisfaÉtion the kind addreſs of the citizens of Newport on my arrival in this State.

Although I am not ...

ADDRESS *from the* HEBREW CONGREGATION. *To the* PRESIDENT *of the* UNITED STATES *of* AMERICA.

SIR,

PERMIT the children of the ſtock of Abraham to approach you, with the moſt cordial affeÉtion and eſteem for your perſon and merits—and to join with our fellow-citizens in welcoming you to Newport.

With pleaſure we reflect on thoſe days—thoſe days of difficulty and danger, when the God of Iſrael, who delivered David from the peril of the ſword, ſhielded your head in the day of battle—And we rejoice to think, that the ſame ſpirit, who reſted in the boſom of the greatly beloved Daniel, enabling him to preſide over the provinces of the Babyloniſh Empire, reſts, and ever will reſt, upon you, enabling you to diſcharge the arduous duties of Chief Magiſtrate in theſe States.

Deprived as we heretofore have been of the invaluable rights of free citizens, we now (with a deep ſenſe of gratitude to the Almighty Diſpoſer of all events) behold a government ereÉted by the MAJESTY OF THE PEOPLE—a government which to bigotry gives no ſanÉtion—to perſecution no aſſiſtance; but generouſly affording to ALL liberty of conſcience, and immunities of citizenſhip—deeming every one, of whatever nation, tongue or language, equal parts of the great governmental machine. This ſo ample and extenſive federal Union, whoſe baſis is philanthropy, mutual confidence, and public virtue, we cannot but acknowledge to be the work of the great God, who ruleth in the armies of Heaven and among the inhabitants of the earth, doing whatſoever ſeemeth him good.

For all the bleſſings of civil and religious liberty which we enjoy under an equal and benign adminiſtration, we deſire to ſend up our thanks to the Ancient of Days, the great Preſerver of men—beſeeching him, that the angel who conduÉted our forefathers through the wilderneſs into the promiſed land, may graciouſly conduÉt you through all the difficulties and dangers of this mortal life; and when, like Joſhua, full of days and full of honour, you are gathered to your fathers, may you be admitted into the Heavenly Paradiſe ...

MOSES SEIXAS, Warden.

The ANSWER.
To the HEBREW CONGREGATION *in* NEW RHODE-ISLAND.

GENTLEMEN,

WHILE I receive with much ſatisfaÉtion your addreſs, replete with expreſſions of affeÉtion and eſteem, I rejoice in the opportunity of aſſuring you, that I ſhall always retain a grateful remembrance of the cordial welcome I experienced in my viſit to Newport from all claſſes of citizens.

The reflection on the days of difficulty and danger which are paſt, is rendered the more ſweet, from a conſciouſneſs that they are ſucceeded by days of uncommon proſperity and ſecurity. If we have wiſdom to make the beſt uſe of the advantages with which we are now favored, we cannot fail, under the juſt adminiſtration of a good government, to become a great and a happy people.

The citizens of the United States of America have a right to applaud themſelves for having given to mankind examples of an enlarged and liberal policy worthy of imitation. ALL poſſeſs alike liberty of conſcience, and immunities of citizenſhip, now no more that toleration is ſpoken of, as if it was by the indulgence of one claſs of people, that another enjoyed the exerciſe of their inherent natural rights. For happily the government of the United States gives to bigotry no ſanÉtion—to perſecution no aſſiſtance, requires only that they who live under its proteÉtion, ſhould demean themſelves as good citizens, in giving it on all occaſions their effeÉtual ſupport.

It would be inconſiſtent with the frankneſs of my charaÉter not to avow, that I am pleaſed with your favourable opinion of my adminiſtration, and fervent wiſhes for my felicity. May the children of the ſtock of Abraham, who dwell in this land, continue to merit and enjoy the good will of the other inhabitants; while every one ſhall ſit in ſafety under his own vine and fig-tree, and there ſhall be none to make him afraid. May the Father of all mercies ſcatter light and gladneſs in our paths, and make us all in our ſeveral vocations uſeful here, and in his own due time and way everlaſtingly happy.

G. WASHINGTON.

ish Empire, rests, and ever will rest, upon you, enabling you to discharge the arduous duties of Chief Magistrate in these states.

Deprived as we heretofore have been of the invaluable rights of free citizens, we now (with a deep sense of gratitude to the Almighty Dispenser of all events) behold a government erected by the majesty of the people, a government which gives to bigotry no sanction, to persecution no assistance; but generously affording to all liberty of conscience and immunities of citizenship, deeming everyone, of whatever nation, tongue, or language, equal parts of the great government machine. This so ample and extensive Federal Union whose basis is philanthropy, mutual confidence and public virtue, we cannot but acknowledge to be the work of the great God who ruleth in the armies of Heaven and among the inhabitants of the earth, doing whatever seemeth Him good.

For all these blessings of civil and religious liberty, which we enjoy under an equal benign administration, we desire to send up our thanks to the ancient of days, the Great Preserver of Man, beseeching Him that the Angel who conducted our forefathers through the wilderness into the promised land may graciously conduct you through all the difficulties and dangers of this mortal life, and when, like Joshua, full of days and full of honor, you are gathered to your fathers, may you be admitted into the Heavenly Paradise to partake of the water of life and the tree of immortality.

Done and signed by the order of the Hebrew Congregation in Newport, R.I., August 17, 1790.

Moses Seixas
Warden

Washington Papers, Library of Congress

I Am a Jew

*In his early twenties, Benjamin Nones traveled to America from France
and soon became a volunteer soldier in the revolutionary war. He fought
with great gallantry through many campaigns on the southern front.
But his services did not make him immune from anti-Semitic slander.
Early in August of 1800, a conservative paper,* Gazette of the United
States, *printed a nasty unsigned letter libeling Nones and blacks, working people, and the poor in general.*

*The editor of the paper refused to print Nones's reply, whereupon
Nones sent it to* The Philadelphia Aurora, *which ran it on August
13, 1800. It is a passionate self-defense by a man accused of being a
Jew, a radical, and poor.*

. . . I AM A JEW. I glory in belonging to that persuasion,
which even its opponents, whether Christian, or Mahomedan, allow to be of divine origin—of that persuasion on
which Christianity itself was originally founded, and must
ultimately rest—which has preserved its faith secure and
undefiled for near three thousand years, whose votaries
have never murdered each other in religious wars, or cherished the theological hatred so general, so unextinguishable
among those who revile them. A persuasion, whose patient
followers have endured for ages the pious cruelties of Pa-
gans, and of Christians, and persevered in the unoffending
practice of their rites and ceremonies, amidst poverties and
privations; amidst pains, penalities, confiscations, banishments, tortures, and deaths; beyond the example of any
other sect which the page of history has hitherto recorded.

To be of such a persuasion is to me no disgrace; though
I well understand the inhuman language of bigoted contempt, in which your reporter by attempting to make me
ridiculous, as a Jew, has made himself detestable, whatever

Benjamin Nones' reply to an anti-Semitic attack was published in THE
PHILADELPHIA AURORA *on August 13, 1800.*

The Philadelphia Aurora:

SURGO UT PROSIM.

PHILADELPIA:

WEDNESDAY, AUGUST 13, 1800.

TO THE EDITOR.

Mr. Duane.

I enclose you an article which I deem ed it but justice to my character to pre sent for insertion in the Gazette of the United States, in reply to some illiberali ties which were thrown out against me in common with many a respectable citi zens in that paper of the 5 h inst. When I presented it to Mr. Wayne, he promis ed me in the presence of a third person, that he would publish it. I waited until this day, when finding it had not appear ed, I called on him, when he informed me that he would not publish it. I tendered h m payment if he should require it. His business appears to be so adverse and shut the door against justification. I need not say more:

I am &c.   B. NONES.
Philadelphia Aug. 11, 1800.

To the Printer of the Gazette of the U. S.
SIR,

I hope, if you take the liberty of insert ing calumnies against individuals, for the amusement of your readers, you will at least have so much regard to justice, as to permit the injured through the same chan nel that conveyed the slander, to appeal to the public in self defence.——I ex

I am accused of being a *Jew*; of being a *Republican*: and of being *Poor*.

I am a *Jew*. I glory in belonging to that persuasion, which even its opponents, whether Christian, or Mahomedan, allow to be of divine origin —of that persuasion on which christianity itself was originally founded, and must ultimately rest—which has preserved its faith secure and undefi led, for near three thousand years—whose votaries have never murdered each other in religious wars, or cherished the theolo gical hatred so general, so inextinguish able among those who revile them. A per

suasion, whose patient followers have en dured for ages the pious cruelties of Pa gans, and of christians, and persevered in the unoffending practice of their rites an ceremonies, amidst poverty and priva tions—amidst pains, penalties, confiscations banishments, tortures, and deaths, beyond the example of any other sect, which the page of history has hitherto recorded.

To be of such a persuasion, is to me no disgrace; but I well understand the inhu man language, of bigotted contempt, in which your reporter by attempting to make me ridiculous, as a Jew, has made himself detestable, whatever religious persuasion may be dishonored by his adherence.

But I am a Jew. I am so—and so were Abraham, and Isaac, and Moses and the prophets, and so too were Christ and his apostles. I feel no disgrace in ranking with such society, however, it may be subject to the illiberal buffoonery of such men as your correspondent.

I am a Republican! Thank God I have. And I have no other rea son, for that reason am I a republican. Among the pious priesthood of church establishments, we are compassionately ranked with Turks, Infidels, and Heretics. In the monarchies of Europe, we are hunt ed from society—stigmatized as unworthy of common civility, thrust out as it were from the converse of men; objects of mockery and insult to froward children, the butts of vulgar wit, and low buffoonery, such as your correspondent Mr. Wayne is not ashamed to set us an example of. Among the nations of Europe, we are in habitants indeed every where—but Citi zens no where unless in Republics. Here, in France, and in the Batavian Republic alone, are we treated as men, and as bre thren. In republics we have rights, in monarchies we live but to experience wrongs. And why? because we and our forefathers have not sacrificed our princi ples to our interest, or earned an exemp tion from pain and poverty, by the der liction of our religious duties, no wonder we are objects of derision to those, who have no principles, moral or religious to guide their conduct.

How then can a Jew but be a Republi can? in America particularly. Unfeeling & ungrateful would he be, if he were callous to the glorious and benevolent cause of the difference between his situation in this land of freedom, and among the proud and privileged law givers of Eu rope.

religious persuasion may be dishonored by his adherence.

But I am a Jew. I am so; and so were Abraham, and Isaac, and Moses and the prophets, and so too were Christ and his apostles; and I feel no disgrace in ranking with such society, however it may be subject to the illiberal buffoonery of such men as your correspondents.

I am a REPUBLICAN! Thank God I have not been so heedless and so ignorant of what has passed, and is now passing in the political world. I have not been so proud or so prejudiced as to renounce the cause for which I have FOUGHT, as an American, throughout the whole of the revolutionary war, in the militia of Charleston, and in Pulaski's legion. I fought in almost every action which took place in Carolina, and in the disastrous affair of Savannah, shared the hardships of that sanguinary day, and for three and twenty years I felt no disposition to change my political any more than my religious principles. And which, in spite of the witling scribblers of aristocracy, I shall hold sacred until death, as not to feel the ardour of republicanism. . . .

On religious grounds I am a republican. Kingly government was first conceded to the foolish complaints of the Jewish people as a punishment and a curse; and so it was to them until their dispersion, and so it has been to every nation who have been as foolishly tempted to submit to it. Great Britain hast a king, and her enemies need not wish her the sword, the pestilence, and the famine. . . .

I am a Jew, and if for no other reason, for that reason am I a republican. Among the pious priesthood of church establishments, we are compassionately ranked with Turks, Infidels and Heretics. In the MONARCHIES of Europe we are hunted from society, stigmatized as unworthy of common civility, thrust out as it were from the converse of men; objects of mockery and insult to froward children, the butts of vulgar wit and low buffoonery, such as your correspon-

24

dent, Mr. Wayne, is not ashamed to set us an example of. Among the nations of Europe we are inhabitants everywhere; but citizens nowhere UNLESS IN REPUBLICS. Here, in France and in the Batavian republic alone, we are treated as men and as brethren. In republics we have RIGHTS, in monarchies, live but to experience WRONGS. And why? Because we and our forefathers have not sacrificed our principles to our interest, or earned an exemption from pain and poverty, by the dereliction of our religious duties; no wonder we are objects of derision to those, who have NO principles, moral or religious, to guide their conduct.

How then can a Jew but be a Republican? In America particularly. Unfeeling and ungrateful would he be if he were callous to the glorious and benevolent cause of the difference between his situation in this land of freedom and among the proud and privileged law-givers of Europe.

But I am POOR; I am so, my family also is large, but soberly and decently brought up. They have not been taught to revile a Christian because his religion is not SO OLD as theirs. They have not been taught to mock even at the errors of good intention, and conscientious belief. I trust that they will always leave this to men as unlike themselves as I hope I am to your scurrilous correspondent.

I know that to purse-proud aristocracy poverty is a crime, but it may sometimes be accompanied with honesty even in a Jew; I was bankrupt some years ago; I obtained by certificate and was discharged from my debts. Having been more successful afterwards, I called my creditors together, and eight years afterwards, unsolicited, I discharged all my old debts. I offered interest which was refused by my creditors, and they gave me from under their hands, without any solicitations of mine, as a testimonial of the fact (to use their own language) "as a tribute due to my honor and honesty. . . ." The public will now judge who is the proper object of ridicule and contempt, your facetious reporter, or

> Your humble servant,
> Benjamin Nones

Philadelphia, August 11, 1800

The Philadelphia Aurora, August 13, 1800

A Reproof
to Henry Clay

One of Maryland's prominent Jewish citizens, Solomon Etting, was vigilant on behalf of equal rights for Jews. In his home state, which was notorious for denying Jews such rights, Etting led the fight for many years to change state law so that persons "professing the Jewish religion" could hold office. When his campaign succeeded in 1826, he and Jacob Cohen were elected to the city council of Baltimore.

In this letter, Etting calls Senator Henry Clay of Kentucky to account for what could have been understood as an anti-Semitic remark made during a debate in the U.S. Senate. Clay apologized the next day.

Baltimore, July 15th, 1832

DEAR SIR: You know that I am your friend, and therefore I write to you freely. Several of the religious society to which I belong, myself included, feel both surprised and hurt by the manner in which you introduce the expression "the Jew" in debate in the Senate of the United States,

26

evidently applying it as a reproachful designation of a man whom you considered obnoxious in character and conduct.

I do not know the person you allude to; the term "the Jew" as used by you, is considered illiberal. If therefore, you have no antipathy to the people of that religious society, I can readily believe you will have no objection to explain to me by a line, what induced the expression.

I am, with respect and esteem,
Your Obt. St.
S. Etting

Hon. H. Clay,
United States Senate, Washington.

Jacob R. Marcus, *Sourcebook for American Jewish History*

Not Two Dollars
in Two Days

In 1842 a young Jewish peddler from Bavaria, Germany, arrived in New York. He was one of thousands of Bavarian Jews swept up by an America fever at that time.

For centuries Europe's Jews had been confined to the ghetto. Then under the banners of the French Revolution, carried across the continent by Napoleon's armies, the Jews had been emancipated. Napoleon's new Civil Code had protected their life, property, and religious freedom. But with the fall of Napoleon, old fences were erected again. In Germany the Jews lost all they had gained and were burdened with special taxes and restrictions on occupations. Bavaria even set a quota on the number of Jewish marriages that could take place.

So this young man, with his brother Moses, crossed the Atlantic in search of a better life. He did not find it easy going. The hardship and homesickness he records in his diary were common to many pioneer peddlers, who came with no money and no connections. This diarist crisscrossed New England. Other peddlers plunged West, tracing the paths of hunters and homesteaders into the vast interior, bearing on their backs the household goods the settlers needed.

I was in New York, trying in vain to find a job as clerk in a store. But business was too slow, and I had to do as all the others; with a bundle on my back, I had to go out into the country, peddling various articles. This, then, is the vaunted luck of the immigrants from Bavaria! O misguided fools, led astray by avarice and cupidity! You have left your friends and acquaintances, your relatives and your parents, your home and your fatherland, your language and your customs, your faith and your religion—only to sell your wares in the wild places of America, in isolated farmhouses and tiny hamlets. . . .

In such an existence the single man gets along far better than the father of a family. Such fools as are married not only suffer themselves, but bring suffering to their women. How must an educated woman feel when after a brief stay at home, her supporter and shelterer leaves with his pack on his back, not knowing where he will find lodging on the next night. . . .

Last week in the vicinity of Plymouth I met two peddlers, Lehman and Marx. Marx knew me from Furth [Germany], and that night we stayed together at a farmer's house. After supper we started singing while I felt melancholy and depressed. O, how I thought of my dear mother while I sang!

Today, Sunday, October 16th, we are here in North Bridgewater [Massachusetts], and I am not so downcast as I was two weeks ago. The devil has settled 2,000 shoemakers here, who do not have a cent of money. Suppose, after all, I were a soldier in Bavaria; that would have been a bad lot. I will accept three years in America instead. But I could not stand it any longer.

As far as the language is concerned, I am getting along pretty well. But I don't like to be alone. The Americans are a peculiar people. Although they sit together by the dozen in taverns, they turn their backs to each other, and no one talks to anybody else. Is this supposed to be the custom of a republic? I don't like it. Is this supposed to be the fashion of the nineteenth century? I don't like it either. . . .

On Wednesday, November 9th, . . . [my brother] Moses and I went to Holden, where we stayed until Sunday . . . with Mr. How. On Monday we went on, arriving on Tuesday at Rutland. In the morning our packs seemed very heavy, and we had to rest every half-mile. In the afternoon a buggy was offered to us and, thank Heaven, it was within our means. We took off our bundles and anticipated thriving business. . . .

Winter has come because there is much snow and wind since Thursday, the 24th. We were at Sterling and Leominster on Monday, November 28th, and went from there to Lunenburg.

Not far from here we were forced to stop on Wednesday, November 30th, because of the heavy snow. We sought to spend the night with a cooper, a Mr. Spaulding, but his wife did not wish to take us in. She was afraid of strangers; she might not sleep well; we should go our way. And outside there raged the worst blizzard I have ever seen. O God, I thought, is this the land of liberty and hospitality and tolerance? . . .

After we had talked to this woman for half an hour, after repeatedly pointing out that to turn us forth into the blizzard would be sinful, we were allowed to stay. She became friendlier, indeed, after a few hours, and at night she even joined us in singing. But how often I remembered during that evening how my poor mother treated strangers at all times. Every poor man, every traveler who entered the house, was welcomed hospitably and given the best at our table. Her motto, even for strangers, was: "Who throws stones at me shall be, in turn, pelted by me with bread." Now her own children beg for shelter in a foreign land. . . .

Thursday was a day of rest owing to twelve inches of snow. On Friday and Saturday business was very poor, and we did not take in $2 during the two days. . . .

American Jewish Archives, III, 1951

Coming to Our Aid

It was the mass emigration of the German Jews in the first half of the 19th century that perhaps saved American Jewry from disappearing as an ethnic group. Its members had been very few and very isolated from one another by distance and poor communications. Unlike many other immigrant groups, Jews had come not from one country, but from many. They spoke different languages and were raised in different cultures.

In America they had free choice in religion. No church forced them to convert. They could maintain their faith, enter into another, or simply give up altogether their Jewish connection. Many melted into the new society.

With the coming of the German Jews in great numbers, there was a much better chance to build a strong Jewish community. The Germans formed synagogues and opened parochial schools. For the Jews who needed

Henry Jones, one of the dozen founders of B'nai B'rith, in a drawing by George Peixotto.

help, they could provide clothing, food, fuel, loans, jobs, education, aid for the sick and orphaned, and burial services.

The comradeship they felt was expressed in many ways. One was the founding in 1843 of the first Jewish fraternal society in the world— B'nai B'rith (Children of the Covenant). It was organized by a dozen poor German Jews in New York. The society brought Jews together for mutual aid, for education, for social service. Soon it had branches in most of the nation's Jewish communities.

This is the Preamble to B'nai B'rith's Constitution.

B'nai B'rith has taken upon itself the mission of uniting Israelites in the work of promoting their highest interests and those of humanity; of developing and elevating the mental and moral character of the people of our faith; of inculcating the purest principles of philanthropy, honor and patriotism; of supporting science and art; alleviating the wants of the poor and needy; visiting and attending the sick; coming to the rescue of victims of persecution; providing for, protecting and assisting the widow and orphan on the broadest principles of humanity.

Preamble to the Constitution of the Independent Order B'nai B'rith, 1843

A Terrible Fire
of Artillery

At sixteen, Jacob Hirschorn was walking the streets of New York looking for work. It was the year 1846, and the Jewish youngster had just arrived alone from Bavaria. He found a job at last—soldiering in the American army, now at war with Mexico. Although only a boy, below military age, he was accepted as a volunteer. Jacob was put aboard General Winfield Scott's invasion fleet, which sailed south to make an unopposed landing at Vera Cruz. Jacob saw action for almost two years, through the capture of Mexico City and the end of the war.

Many Americans bitterly opposed the Mexican War as an unjust war. They considered it an act of aggression against a neighbor, one that was designed to expand slave territory and to increase the slaveholders' power in government. Jacob's recollections of his part in the war never go into the politics behind it, but the details he provides portray

---

Our encampment outside of Vera Cruz was a terribly trying one, for the Northers as they blew in from the sea, over the sand hills in which we camped, caused immense suffering. The sand nearly blinded us. Our bodies, our food, our drinking water, all were covered with sand and dirt. Especially the water, which at best was a little dirty warm mush obtained by digging into the sand about a foot or so. We were glad when orders arrived to strike tents and march inland towards Jalapa.

At Cerro Gordo we found Santa Anna entrenched on the heights with 20,000 troops and any amount of artillery. We had to pass there, no other way being passable; therefore, General Scott ordered, the next day at sunrise, an assault on the fortified heights. Step by step we had to pull our guns up by ropes. Forty or fifty men, attached with one hand to the rope, and with the other hand getting a hold on some grass cactus or any other old things, so as to keep a footing and not to roll down again, with gun and all, and the Mexicans, continually firing on us, from above. It was a terrible battle, but after six hours fighting we conquered and the Mexicans fled, "vamoosed" as they call it. . . .

By easy marches, we reached Pueblo. . . . About half our force were invalids, some killed and wounded in battle and a great many sick at the hospitals as a result of eating the fruits of the country, which our boys could not stand. We had to wait for reinforcements, mail and supplies, before we could attempt to attack Santa Anna, entrenched in every conceivable shape, defending the city of Mexico. . . .

Being able to converse in English, German and French, I was from the start transferred to the quartermaster's department. Because I was a minor, I could not get a regular commission in the army as an officer, but they would send me out in the country at the head of a company of dragoons or mounted riflemen and six or eight wagons, to scout and forage for anything eatable for man or beast. The country had a good many French and Swiss settlers, with whom I could converse, and so I always managed to bring in something. . . .

After a sojourn of about three months at Pueblo, the order was given to march and we moved on to the capital, the city of Mexico, with an army mustering about 12,000 men fit for duty.

The first battle took place at Contreras, where we encountered a part of the Mexican army. . . . My brigade, then under the command of General Franklin Pierce, consisting of the New York and South Carolina volunteers, was ordered to attack. We formed in a hacienda, about one and a half miles from the Mexican line fortifications in an open cornfield and at the first fire of the Mexicans about one percent of the Palmetto boys and about the same number of our regiment fell, killed or wounded. . . .

We marched through the open field not minding their shots at all, reached a trench, which we filled with dead horses and mules, crossed over and attacked them with the bayonet. That was more than they could stand. They began to waver. Worth forced the bridge, Santa Anna ran for his life and his defeated army followed him pell-mell, and we after them to be revenged for our dead and wounded comrades. Oh! What a glorious sight it was to see Phil Kearney at the head of his dragoons, riding into them and the infantry following up. . . .

General Scott ordered an advance into the city of Mexico. Molina del Rey, an outwork near Chapultepec, was attacked first and carried. Next Chapultepec, the West Point of Mexico, built on a steep hill and surrounded by a high wall, well defended by Mexicans and splendidly supported by the cadets, was to be assaulted. Here a call for volunteers from the different regiments was made to serve under the command of Major Twiggs, which command was called the "Forlorn Hope," because none of them ever expected to return alive.

We advanced two hundred strong. I omitted to say that I volunteered to join. Under a terrible fire of artillery and muskets from the castle and wall, we approached the wall, raised our ladders, and began to climb up. It was a terrible sight to see our brave fellows drop from the ladders, shot. Finally we reached the top of the wall. . . .

As soon as the glorious "Stars and Stripes" floated from the wall, the Mexican flag came down. The defenders became demoralized and vamoosed. . . . While the assault on the wall took place our siege guns, mortars and others poured shells and round shot into the castle, which, after a while, set the castle on fire. Then the complete rout of that portion of the Mexican army took place. Having possession of the castle situated about three miles from the city, we advanced on the city. Our division, [which] was to attack the Garrita del Belen, were behind the breastworks. The Mexicans fought bravely; we forced them back however, and finally entered the city, opposed by the retreating enemy, who defended every foot of ground stubbornly and who were nobly assisted by hundreds of Mexican ladies, who from the tops of their houses (all flat tops) were pouring boiling water, boiling oil, rocks, anything they could lay their hands on, upon the very much exposed heads of our boys. Finally about four o'clock P.M. we reached the "Plaza," the principal square of the city, planted the American flag on top of the Halls of Montezuma, the palace of Mexico, and Gen. Scott established his headquarters therein.

The American Israelite, Vol 50, No. 3, July 16, 1903

Fifty Canoes with Indian Chiefs

Jews were often among the first permanent settlers in the new lands of the West. Jewish trappers and fur traders sometimes made the first surveys of strange territory. Some married Indian women, some became Indian scouts, some founded new towns in remote places. As Western cities leaped ahead in population, the size of their Jewish communities grew too. By 1850 there were 200 Jewish families in Chicago and as many in Milwaukee.

There were great risks in trading on the frontier. Mining camps, where the peddlers sold their wares, could turn into ghost towns overnight. Peddlers were robbed by bandits, died of fevers, froze to death, were killed in Indian wars. But Indians and Jews often had a peaceable connection. The Jew was the Indian's link to the settlers; the Indian provided skins for the Jewish trader. Many Jews learned Indian languages well enough to serve as interpreters at army posts.

In the 1840s, Augusta Levy, a German Jew, and her husband John Meyer Levy, an English Jew, were living on the Wisconsin frontier. He was a trader doing good business with the Indians. The federal government, however, ordered the Indians to move out of the region, and many of the white settlers left too. The Levys decided to stay. In her memoirs Augusta tells of watching an Indian council, called when the Indians were resisting the removal order.

Most of the Indians were still scattered around in Minnesota. They liked this country so well they refused to leave till they were taken by force, which was done about the middle of May. They begged my husband to allow all the chiefs to meet at our house for a council. He allowed them to come but told them they must keep sober and behave themselves. They promised faithfully, and left satisfied.

Next day about eleven o'clock, a beautiful, bright day, we could see a great way up and down the river; all at once we saw the greatest sight I ever saw. About fifty canoes appeared, filled with all the Indian chiefs, all of them dressed and painted, and with big bunches of feathers on their heads and tomahawks in their hands. They were dressed in their best, and glistened as if a procession all shining with gold and silver was coming down the river.

I didn't know anything about their arrangements, so little Willie and I were scared. We feared that they were coming to kill us all. I ran to shut all the windows and lock all the doors. We were alone in the house. Then we hid ourselves in a dark room. I couldn't keep myself in hiding. You know how it is with women, even if they think there

A Jewish trader on the Western frontier, photographed with Indians while doing business in Omaha, Nebraska, in the 1870s. NEBRASKA STATE HISTORICAL SOCIETY

is danger, they want to see everything. I saw the Indians had landed from their canoes, in front of our house, by the river bank. I marked them all as they landed safely and as they came marching directly up towards our house I became alarmed again, and ran back into my hiding place.

They knocked and knocked but I would not open the door. Then I heard someone pounding and pounding, and kicking against the door. This noise was not by moccasins but by boots. Then someone tried to break in the door. Then I heard swearing, in English and German, but I wouldn't open the door. Finally my husband came around to the kitchen window and called my name. Then of course I thought I was all right, and quickly came out of my corner. I asked him if he didn't see the Indians around by the front door. They were all there, with their tomahawks, to kill us. He said "Open the doors quickly, in Heaven's name! What did you lock yourself in for?" Said I, "Didn't you see the Indians at the front door to kill us?" Said he, "If you don't open the doors, quick, I'll kick them in!" So I opened the kitchen door to let him in and he went to the front door at once to let the Indians in, while I hastened back to my hiding place.

If there was any scalping to be done, I thought they could take him first. But they all went very quietly into the dining room, sat down on the floor, had a smoke all around, and then they asked for some water. My husband called me to bring in a pail of water and a pint cup, that he would stay in sight. I told him to take the pint cup, and the Indians, and take them down to the river and water them down there. Our hired man made his appearance just then and he was sent to the river after the water, because we didn't have any well. After this I got up courage enough, as I didn't see any scalping done, to peep in.

As I say, they sat all around the room, and there wasn't a clean spot to be seen anywhere. They had used it for a spittoon, continually. I felt mad enough now to go down to the river and get water enough to drown them all out. My husband saw I was excited, so he took me into the other room and told me to have patience. After the council was over and they had left, he would get a couple of men and have the room cleaned. They took a smoke all around again and then shook hands and departed. I wished them a pleasant journey, and never to return.

They got my husband to write to Washington to ask the government to take the treaty back. They liked it so well here that they did not want to go to the new home the government had provided for them. They waited till my husband got an answer from Washington. They were in hopes that they could stay but were refused, and had to leave the country, mighty quick. It was very lonely in La Crosse after so many of our best settlers left.

By June the Indians had all left for St. Paul. . . .

Augusta Levy, *Reminiscences,* in the Archives Division, the State Historical Society of Wisconsin

Sharks, Fires, and Gold Nuggets

When he was fourteen, Morris Schloss embarked on a series of adventures that carried him from the Poland of his birth to the California of the gold rush days. He left his family for England in 1842. After five years knocking about Birmingham, he took passage for New York. His restless spirit sent him roaming again six months later, and he sailed on a ship heading down the Atlantic for the tip of South America and then up the Pacific for the gold fields of California. Morris was a little dark-skinned man scarcely five foot high, with only one eye to see his way through trouble. He would live to be eighty-five, surviving almost as many trials as Samson.

We pick up his autobiography as his ship rounds Cape Horn, enroute to the West Coast.

After rounding Cape Horn, and when near Valparaiso, one very hot day, I jumped overboard into the Pacific Ocean for a swim. A sailor aloft sang out: "A shark in sight." I hurried up to the ship, a line was thrown to me, and I was hauled up.

Fifteen minutes later a monster shark twelve feet long was caught, cut to pieces by the sailors, and thrown back into the water again. . . .

[I] arrived in San Francisco, September 25, 1849, landing at the foot of Broadway Street with my baggage.

I brought with me a wagon packed in a large box and, at the landing, a man asked me what was in the box. I told him, a wagon, and he asked the price of it. I answered $125, and he offered me $100, which rather surprised me, as the man had not seen the contents of the box. I accepted his offer, and he paid me in gold dust. I had only paid $15 for this wagon in New York, so I thought this was rather a good beginning for me.

The man was very careful in opening the box not to break the lid, and then, taking out the wagon, he said to me: "Stranger, you may keep the wagon, for I only want the box" (for which I had paid $3). "That case is what I want," he said. "I am a cobbler, and in the daytime it will be my shop, and at night, my residence." That box measured seven feet by four feet.

I then removed my baggage to Jackson Street, invested $100 in stationery which I exhibited in Portsmouth Square, then called the Plaza. I sold my stationery at a profit of

500 percent and made money very fast.

I was then introduced by a friend to the proprietor of the El Dorado gambling house, a big tent on the southeast corner of Washington and Kearny Streets, to play music every evening, from seven to ten o'clock, for one ounce ($16), and from ten to eleven, extra pay of a grab, which meant a handful of silver from the monte table. About the middle of October, I rented a store on Washington Street, next to the El Dorado, four and one-half feet by twenty-five feet, for $400 per month. [I] speculated in buying trunks from passengers who were wild to go to the mines, and I made money faster than I ever expected to. In short, I made, in seven or eight weeks, between $5,000 and $6,000.

Then a fire, the first in the city, broke out in the Parker House, back of my store, and as I had scattered [gun] powder all over my store, I had to run for my life, and lost all I had made since my arrival in the city. That fire spread over the block from Washington to Clay and from Kearny to Montgomery Streets.

I then engaged passage on the ship *Galinda* for Trinidad Bay [California]. There was great excitement and a rush in that direction, caused by the reports that nuggets of gold had been found scattered all along the bay shore. When I landed, I found Digger Indians, but no signs of gold and no ship to return on; so I had to remain there four months, living on beans, crackers, and clams, the latter being very plentiful on the beach and easily found. Finally, a schooner brought me back to San Francisco, and I started in business again, and made money. . . .

I kept a store in Shasta. We organized a secret order here, called Iclapsus Vitus, which consisted of judges, lawyers, doctors, merchants, and in fact the best element in the county.

After a year or so, we gave a grand ball in a large stable,

41

illuminated with many tallow candles. The attendance was about 100 men to one lady. The music consisted of a fiddle and a banjo. To engage a partner for a dance was out of the question. I ventured to ask a Spanish girl for a dance, telling her my name was on her program. She coolly told me that I was a liar. That was the etiquette of those bygone days. . . .

In 1852, after being in business for three months, the greatest fire that ever occurred in San Francisco swept everything clean from California Street to Telegraph Hill, and from Dupont Street to Battery Street. I lost everything by this fourth fire, and I had not a cent of insurance, as there was not an insurance company in San Francisco at that time. . . .

In 1853, I opened a store in Redding, Shasta County, and did very well. [I] made plenty of money in the ensuing two years, when a big fire broke out and the whole town was laid in ashes. I lost over $16,000, but managed to bring stock up again from San Francisco, although it took me six weeks to do so, for the Sacramento Valley was under water.

On my arrival with my goods, I was waited upon by a committee and told not to sell more than one pair of boots and one pair of blankets to each man, as there was no hope for any more goods to come in for the winter.

I again made a raise [stake], sold out, and left for San Francisco. I sent for my girl, got married, and settled down at last. . . .

I then joined the Vigilance Committee [and] held a gun in my hand when Casey and Cora were hung. Was on guard in Fort Gunnybags at the time that Judge [David Smith] Terry was a prisoner [for knifing a Vigilante agent] and [Terry] came very near being hung. And [I was on guard] at the time that Yankee Sullivan committed suicide by cutting his arm. And when, late in 1856, over 5,000

Vigilante Committeemen had a grand march and demonstration, we dispersed the thieves. Then we elected honest judges, banished all ballot box stuffers, and San Francisco was saved.

Jacob R. Marcus, *Memoirs of American Jews*, Vol. II (KTAV, 1974)

The Chicago of 1850

Chicago in 1850 was a city of 30,000 people. Only a tiny number were Jews. One of these was Leopold Mayer. At twenty-three he had just arrived to join two of his older brothers who had earlier emigrated from their small town in Germany. To young Leopold, America was "the promised land of freedom, where the laws, at least, are the same for Jews as for non-Jews." Fresh from a land where anti-Semitism was powerful and open, he said, "The stigma of inequality burned in me like a fiery coal."

Nearly a half-century later—and now a banker—Leopold Mayer talked to the local Council of Jewish Women of what life was like for a Jew in the Chicago of the 1850s.

April 23, 1850, when I came to Chicago, the Jews numbered possibly 200. The congregation had 28 contributing members, and on the very first day I was introduced to most of them, including the president and minister. . . . The duties of a minister were manifold. He was the reader, he had to perform the marriage ceremony, he had to be present at funerals and read the prayer there as well as in the house of mourning, he had to act as shochet—that is, to kill cattle and fowl according to Jewish rite and custom.

43

Instruction in both the tenets and the morals of Judaism were lacking. Every Jew was his own teacher and rabbi. A religious school for children was not necessary, as there were but few children of school age here. . . .

Our people were far from being a political unit. Some were hard-shell Democrats and some were ardent Whigs; Free-Soilers, there were hardly any. My first political knowledge came from the Free-Soilers, and I readily adopted their doctrines, as they coincided closely with the ideas of liberty I had imbibed in Germany during the stormy times of '48.

The relations between Jews and non-Jews were cordial, and many of the former not only belonged to the various political and fraternal organizations, but also held offices therein. Numbers belonged to the volunteer fire department, and Henry Greenebaum was captain of engine company No. 6 when he was scarcely 21 years old. The balls and festivities given by the non-Jews were often attended by the Jews, who were never in the least looked upon as undesirable. The Germans, Jews, and non-Jews were one, and the prejudices from the fatherland, if not dead, were at least hidden. For myself, I must say that I was made welcome in every American household in which I had scholars or where I had been introduced. I was invited to all the parties given by the young people of my acquaintance, and it was to an American lady that I owed my success.

Among the Jews themselves social entertainments gradually increased in number as the number of young men and women grew. Engagements were still few, but the young folks longed for diversion. In summer, carriage rides and joint walks in the fields, and in winter, sleigh-rides were in order; sometimes there were even theatre parties given.

The visiting day was Sunday, and it was always prearranged at whose house the following Sunday should be spent. There were no whist nor poker parties—as yet, the ladies did not play cards. Dances, today called balls, were difficult to arrange; but we had them. . . .

The Jews in Chicago were fairly well situated. . . . Some had dry goods, others clothing stores; many were engaged in the cigar and tobacco business, and there were already a plumber and joiner, and even a carpenter here. Some— loading their goods upon a wagon, others upon their shoulders—followed the honorable vocation of peddling.

The houses in which we lived in those days in Chicago were modest one- or two-story frame dwellings. . . . The dietary laws were strictly observed and the Sabbath and festivals were celebrated with Jewish rites. Business houses were at no great distance from the homes and the men were generally to be found with their families after business hours. The women occupied themselves with needlework, household duties, and reading. The children were reared to honor and obey their parents. . . . If the Jewish home was not quite what it was in Germany, it was still founded on filial love and respect.

Chicago Journal, Nov. 14, 1899

I Plead for the Equal Rights of My Sex

One of the early advocates of equal rights for women was Ernestine Rose. Born in 1810 in a Polish ghetto, the daughter of a rabbi, she rebelled early against the traditional position of women. At sixteen, when her mother died, she went to court to prevent her father from forcing her to marry a man she did not love. For the next five years,

Ernestine Rose, an immigrant from Poland, depicted in a popular engraving of the 1850s, when she crisscrossed America speaking for the antislavery and women's rights movements.

she traveled through Europe, pleading the cause of human rights.

In 1836, she moved to New York with her husband William Rose. Within a few months, her energy and her eloquence had made her a leader in the campaign for women's rights—this at a time when women met indifference, ridicule, or violence for daring to speak on a public platform. With Susan B. Anthony, Sojourner Truth, Lucretia Mott, Elizabeth Cady Stanton, and others, Ernestine Rose helped organize the women of America into a great force for social and political change.

At the third National Woman's Rights Convention in Syracuse, New York, in 1852, Ernestine Rose made a speech. These brief passages are taken from it.

I am an example of the universality of our claims; for not American women only, but a daughter of poor, crushed Poland, and the downtrodden and persecuted people called the Jews, "a child of Israel" pleads for the equal rights of her sex. . . .

Woman is a slave, from the cradle to the grave. Father, guardian husband—master still. One conveys her, like a piece of property, over to the other. She is said to have been created only for man's benefit, not for her own. This falsehood is the main cause of her inferior education and position. Man has arrogated to himself the right to her person, her property, and her children; and so vitiated is public opinion that if a husband is rational and just enough to acknowledge the influence of his wife, he is called "henpecked." The term is not very elegant, but it is not of my coining; it is yours, and I suppose you know what it means; I don't. But it is high time these irrationalities are done away, for the whole race suffers by it. In claiming our rights we claim the rights of humanity; it is not for the interest of woman only, but the interest of all. The interest of the sexes cannot be separated—together they must enjoy or suffer—both are one in the race. . . .

I wish to introduce a resolution, and leave it to the action of the Convention:

Resolved, That we ask not for our rights as a gift of charity, but as an act of justice. For it is in accordance with the principles of republicanism that, as woman has to pay taxes to maintain government, she has a right to participate in the formation and administration of it. That as she is amenable to the laws of her country, she is entitled to a voice in their enactment, and to all the protective advantages they can bestow; and as she is as liable as man to all the vicissitudes of life she ought to enjoy the same social rights and privileges. And any difference, therefore, in political, civil and social rights, on account of sex, is in direct violation of the principles of justice and humanity, and as such ought to be held up to the contempt and derision of every lover of human freedom. . . .

Proceedings of the Women's Rights Convention, Held at Syracuse, Sept. 8th, 9th & 10th, Syracuse, 1852

With John Brown in Kansas

As a young Jew in Vienna, August Bondi seemed born to rebel against injustice. He was not yet fifteen when the 1848 revolution against the tyrannical monarchy broke out, but he took up arms in its cause. When the revolt failed, his family fled. They reached America late that year, and within a few months August had taken the side of the abolitionists against slavery. He worked in Saint Louis as a store clerk, a printer's apprentice, a schoolteacher. Then in 1855 he read an appeal to freedom-loving men to rush to Kansas to save that territory from "the curse of slavery."

In Kansas the abolitionist settlers were contending with the proslavery settlers for control of the territory. The slaveholders' "Border Ruffians" fought guerrilla battles with antislavery forces, led by such men as John Brown. Bondi moved to Kansas and there met two other Jews, Jacob Benjamin and Theodore Wiener. All three joined Captain John Brown's small band to fight for a free state.

Years later Bondi recalled the campaign in his autobiography. He tells what happened in late May of 1856, when Brown's men set out on one of their raids against the Border Ruffians.

We started after dark, eleven in number. Capt. Brown carried a saber and a largest size revolver. His sons and Thompson had a revolver, cutlass and a squirrel rifle each. Townsley, an old musket. Wiener, a double-barrelled shot gun. Carpenter, one revolver; myself, a flint lock musket of 1812 pattern. About 4 o'clock on the morning of the 27th of May, we reached the hiding place on Taway Creek which Carpenter had picked out for us. Brown inspected the surroundings, put out guards and appointed reliefs. After a while Carpenter brought in some corn for our horses and a small sack of coarse flour, and Capt. Brown began to prepare breakfast.

We stayed here until Sunday June 1st; during these few days I learned to appreciate the exalted character of my old friend. He showed at all times the most affectionate care for each of us. On the morning of the 28th of May, Ben Cochrane, a settler and member of the Pottawatomie Rifles, joined us. He related that in the last raid the ruffians had burned my cabin, stolen my cattle and plundered Wiener's store; all this had happened in the presence of the U.S. troops, under their commanding officer. Capt. Cook, Company F, 2d U.S. Dragoons, was asked by the settlers to interfere. He refused, saying he had no orders to that effect, but ordered the leader of the Border Ruffian militia to surrender all his prisoners to the U.S. troops.

Fighting between the pro- and antislavery forces in the Kansas Territory during the late 1850s. August Bondi was one of three Jews in John Brown's troop. COLLECTION OF MILTON MELTZER

In the afternoon of that day, Carpenter brought Charles Kaiser, a native of Bavaria, and an old soldier of the Revolution of '49, to our camp. He was extremely well pleased to find in me a member of the old Vienna Legion. . . .

It might have been about nine o'clock in the forenoon when [Captain] Brown stopped near Wiener and me and, having looked through his spy glass for some time, said, "It seems the Missourians have also suffered from our fire; they are leaving one by one; we must never allow that. We must try to surround them; we must compel them to surrender." He then walked down our line, spoke with some of the men, and returned with the Moore boys to where Wiener and myself were posted and beckoned us to follow him.

We five, Capt. Brown, the two Moores, Wiener and myself, ran up a hill south of the Missouri camp. As soon as we had gained a commanding position within two hundred yards of the enemy, Capt. Brown ordered the two Moores to aim with their carbines at horses and mules exclusively, and not to shoot at any men at the time, if it could be avoided, as he wanted to take as many prisoners as possible. The Moore boys, with four shots, killed two mules and two horses, which we could perceive created a great consternation in the Missouri camp, and we saw several leaving.

Now Capt. Brown drew and cocked his revolver and declared that he should advance some twenty yards by himself and if then he should wave his hat, we were to follow; Wiener and me ahead; the Moores to come up more slowly that, if necessary, they could cover our retreat with their carbines. According to previous agreement, our comrades along the Santa Fe road were to run to us as soon as they saw his signal with the hat. Capt. Brown advanced but about twenty steps when he stood, waved his hat and we joined him. Then the Captain and we four behind him, together with the seven along the Santa Fe road, charged against the Missouri camp. Capt. Pate stepped out in front of his men and waved a white handkerchief and called out to Capt. Brown that he was ready to leave. Capt. Brown kept on until within five feet of Capt. Pate and, covering the hostile commander with his revolver, called out, "Unconditional surrender." The rifles slipped from the grasp of the Ruffians and Pate surrendered his sword. Twenty-four well-armed cut-throats laid down their arms; some thirty had run off during the engagement; seven, more or less seriously wounded, lay on the ground.

The booty of the day consisted of thirty stands of U.S. rifles and accoutrements, as many revolvers, thirty saddle horses and equipments, two wagons with their teams, and a large amount of provisions, ammunition and camp equipage. Capt. Pate surrendered his sword and revolver and I, being right by, asked him for the powder flask he carried, and [he] gave it to me. I kept the old 1812 musket I carried at Black Jack with that powder flask like a sacred relic. . . .

Autobiography of August Bondi, 1833–1907 (Galesburg, Illinois, 1910)

Let Them But Remain Good Jews

The present-day city of Newark was once a small town in rural New Jersey. When the Kussys arrived there from Germany in the decade before the Civil War, they settled in a neighborhood side by side with non-Jews from their homeland and with Irish immigrants. Gustav Kussy rose at 3 A.M. to prepare the cuts of meats for his butcher trade. By the time the housewives were up and about, he had his meats in a basket and was trudging from town to town, selling them at the door, while his wife Bella waited on customers in the shop. Through hard work and self-denial, the Kussys saved enough to buy a small house. Soon cousins from Europe arrived, to be bedded and fed and guided into promising trades.

Sarah, one of the Kussys daughters, recalls the religious traditions of their home.

In our home a religious spirit prevailed. Upon entering the house one could tell immediately that he was in a Jewish home. Prominent on one of the walls was a large *mizrekh* (a drawing or picture on the east wall), with the legend in Hebrew, "From the rising of the sun unto its setting, the Lord's name is to be praised," and profusely illustrated with Biblical motives. We were taught little Hebrew prayers before we were able to articulate clearly. We also learned German prayers that mother had repeated as a child and were taught the *brokhes* (blessings) for various occasions.

In her religious efforts, as well as in her household responsibilities, mother soon found an admirable assistant in my sister Bertha. She evidently took complete charge of me in my childhood. For I well remember that it was Bertha who taught me my earliest Hebrew prayers. She also washed and dressed me, curled my hair, made my clothes, and taught me how to read before I entered school.

Father, while not as deeply pious as mother, was nonetheless ardently Jewish. During his early married life he had kept his shop closed on the Sabbath. As the growing neighborhood brought with it increasing business competition, he yielded to the pressure of circumstances and kept it open. When father was fifty-seven, my cousin Siegfried took over the business and father was retired, but only nominally, for he continued daily to assist either Siegfried or my brother Meyer, except on the Sabbath. That day was devoted to the synagogue in the morning, and to Jewish study in the afternoon. In later years all the grandchildren would assemble in father's house on Saturday afternoons and leave only after the *havdole* (the benediction over the wine at the close of the Sabbath).

Even during the years that father attended to business, he never failed on Friday night and Saturday noon to bless his children, chant the *Kidush* (benediction over the wine), *bentsh mezumen* (say Grace after meals in unison), sing psalm 144 Saturday at dusk, and make *havdole*, while we all joined in the singing of *Hamavdil ben kodesh lehol.* We observed the dietary laws as a matter of course, whether at home or elsewhere.

The *seder* (festive ceremonious meal) on Passover was an eagerly anticipated event. Preparations for it began weeks ahead. Even the children were drawn into these activities. We cleaned out boxes and bureau drawers, turned pockets inside out, followed father about as he *batteled khomets* (searched for leavened food on the evening before Passover), helped to change the dishes, prepared the *kharoses* (a condiment of nuts, apples and other spices used at the *seder*), and arranged the *seder* dish.

There were always between twenty and thirty persons at our *seder* table. We chanted the service in unison, led by father's tenor voice, which remained in our ears long after he had departed from this earth. The preparations for the *seder* meant terrific work for mother. Yet she had no sympathy for those who engaged rooms at hotels for the week to avoid the home tasks. They were running away from a *mitsve* (good deed), mother would say reproachfully. For mother the festival was far too brief, the period of observance incommensurate with that of initial preparation.

On *Rosh Hashone* (New Year's Day) it was our custom to write New Year's letters to our parents and place them under their plates on the eve of the festival. This custom has survived among some members of the family to this day.

We had no problems of a Hanukah and Christmas conflict. Hanukah, we felt, was for Jews, and Christmas for Christians. We lit our candles and sang *Maos zur* in unison with father. Mother told us the story of the Maccabees and other tales from the Apocrypha, which she read in a little German book that Grandfather Bloch, who had come to spend his last years with his daughters in America, brought from Osterberg.

Bible stories were our bedtime tales, vividly and graphically told by mother. Long before we entered the religious school we knew the patriarchs Moses, David, and Elijah as living characters. Mother also introduced us to the tales of Grimm and Andersen, but these, we knew, were fairy tales, whereas the Bible stories were "real. . . . "

Father was also a staunch believer in the *mitsve* of *bikur kholi* (visiting the sick). He spent many a night at the bedside of a dying Jew. He knew the meaning of Jewish *rakhmones* (compassion). The poor Russian Jewish family that he housed rent-free for five years could have said much on this subject.

On the whole, generosity to the poor was an old family tradition. When Grandma Kussy, in Europe, had laid aside a sum of money for the poor, as had been her custom, and the latter had not come for it soon, she was disconsolate. Her husband had to comfort her that "the world had evidently become wealthier." The lame Jewish *schnorer* [beggar], who called periodically, was always given a dollar. Mother once accused him of some misdeed. Later, when she discovered her error, she would not rest until she sought him out and with tears in her eyes pleaded for his forgiveness.

We attended the synagogue on Saturday as naturally and regularly as we attended the public school during the week, except that we began to attend the synagogue at a younger age. I cannot recollect when I went for the first time. Father was usually in his pew when services began; we, the children, waited for mother. Father, however, begrudged us the extra hour of sleep, claiming that it was a *kharpe un a bushe* (shame and disgrace) for a father to come to the service unaccompanied by his children.

To my father the Bible was truly the Book of Books. I can still see him poring over one of three large illustrated Hebrew folios, with German translation and commentaries, that comprised his beloved Bible. The volumes became worn with use, but they afforded father a real weekly *oneg shabes* (delight of the Sabbath) throughout the greater part of his life. Father could quote whole pages of the Bible in the original Hebrew and his familiarity with the sacred text provided him with a large Hebrew vocabulary, which enabled him to understand and participate in a Hebrew conversation.

Father had a strong sense of identification with the hopes and aspirations of *klal ysroel,* universal Israel. He was more than just an American Jew; all Israel was his concern, its future as well as its past. I recall a day when father came into the room with an open copy of the *Staatszeitung* in his hand: "I have just read," he said in German, "that a school has been opened in Jaffa, Palestine, with Hebrew as the medium of instruction." Then, with eyes aglow and voice thrilled with emotion, he burst forth, "I would go through fire and water for Israel. Some day it will come," he added prophetically, "that we shall possess Palestine. It may come in a perfectly natural way. We may have to buy the land." Revival of the Hebrew language, Jewish national life, Palestine—the connection was clear to father. And this was before Herzl issued his call to the Jewish people and no one had heard of a Jewish National Fund.

Although my parents worked hard and had certain aspirations for their children, they were not interested in the pursuit of wealth. When my brother Joe left home to enter the University of Pennsylvania, father's parting injunction was: "Always maintain an honorable name." And mother expressed her hopes for us in this way: "My children need not become wealthy. Let them but remain good Jews."

Sarah Kussy, "Reminiscences of Jewish Life in Newark, N.J.," *Yivo Annual,* Vol VI, 1951

An Outrage on All Law and Humanity

At the time the Civil War started, America's Jewish population had grown to some 150,000. Two out of three of them were immigrants. Slavery was the issue that was splitting the country, and Jews, like all others, took sides. In the South, few Jews were planters, but most southern Jews went along with the ways of the slave society. In the North, where the Jewish community was much bigger, most Jews chose the cause of freedom. They answered at once to Lincoln's call for troops. More than 6,000 served in the Union army, 11 reached the rank of general, and 7 Jewish soldiers earned the congressional Medal of Honor.

Despite their contributions to the war effort, Jews still felt the lash

56

of anti-Semitism. Political and military figures on both sides made their prejudices public. The most notorious such episode involved General U. S. Grant. In 1862, Grant, as Union commander in the Tennessee district, issued his infamous Order No. 11, expelling all Jews from the region. Speculators had flooded in to make huge profits out of cotton, corrupting army officers through bribery and secret partnerships in illegal operations. Some of the profiteers were Jews; most were not. But Grant's order blamed the "Jews as a class." Without trial or hearing, he ordered them all out within twenty-four hours. Jews in Paducah, Kentucky, whose families were subject to the order, wired this message to President Lincoln protesting the "inhuman" action. Then their spokesman, Cesar Kaskel, went to Washington to present the true facts to the president. Lincoln listened, and revoked the order at once.

Paducah, Ky., December 29, 1862

Hon. Abraham Lincoln,
President of the United States:

General Orders, No. 11, issued by General Grant at Oxford, Miss., December the 17th, commands all post commanders to expel all Jews, without distinction, within twenty-four hours, for his entire department. The undersigned, good

The text of the anti-Semitic General Order No. 11 issued by direction of General U.S. Grant on December 17, 1862.

GENERAL ORDERS, }   HDQRS. 13TH A. C., DEPT. OF THE TENN.,
No. 11.   }   *Holly Springs, December* 17, 1862.

The Jews, as a class violating every regulation of trade established by the Treasury Department and also department orders, are hereby expelled from the department within twenty-four hours from the receipt of this order.

Post commanders will see that all of this class of people be furnished passes and required to leave, and any one returning after such notification will be arrested and held in confinement until an opportunity occurs of sending them out as prisoners, unless furnished with permit from headquarters.

No passes will be given these people to visit headquarters for the purpose of making personal application for trade permits.

By order of Maj. Gen. U. S. Grant:

             JNO. A. RAWLINS,
             Assistant Adjutant-General.

and loyal citizens of the United States and residents of this town for many years, engaged in legitimate business as merchants, feel greatly insulted and outraged by this inhuman order, the carrying out of which would be the grossest violation of the Constitution and our rights as good citizens under it, and would place us, besides a large number of other Jewish families of this town, as outlaws before the whole world. We respectfully ask your immediate attention to this enormous outrage on all law and humanity, and pray for your effectual and immediate interposition. We would respectfully refer you to the post commander and post adjutant as to our loyalty, and to all respectable citizens of this community as to our standing as citizens and merchants. We respectfully ask for immediate instructions to be sent to the commander of this post.

D. Wolff & Bros.

C. F. Kaskel   J. W. Kaskel

The War of the Rebellion: Official Records, Ser. I, Vol. 17, Pt. 2, Washington, 1887

A Place
for Fair Dealing

"The great California Jew" was the name David Lubin earned as a champion of the farmer's cause the world over. He brought together forty nations to form an international institute for raising the living standards of farmers. But in the 1870s, long before that day, he was a young Polish immigrant trying to earn his way selling dry goods in California. David hated the ancient system of salesman and customer haggling over prices, with the customer usually worsted: "I could not

---

I resolved to go up the river to Sacramento and see what chances there were in the state capital.

I went by boat, landing in Sacramento with my share of the stock, and pretty poor stuff it was too. After looking around I found a place I thought would do, on a corner of K Street, above a basement saloon. It was about 10 feet wide by 12 feet deep, separated by a thin partition from a Chinese laundry. I occupied one half. Under me was the saloon; and under the saloon was a pool of stagnant water. On the other corner there was another saloon, and yet another on the third corner.

Well, I settled in and made shelves and painted them, set up a counter made of dry-goods boxes covered with oilcloth, and hung out a sign "D. Lubin, ONE PRICE." I used to get my meals for "two bits" on the floor above me where there was a boarding place, and a sloppy place it was too. I rigged up a bunk in the store, under the counter, and slept there. It took "some" strength to take it apart later on; it was fastened together with spikes and would have stood the weight of an ox, let alone a man. I had a straw mattress and turned in there of nights.

I can assure you I had a pretty tough time; but I ran things according to my own ideas of what was right, and stuck to them; fixed prices marked in plain figures, and no lying as to the quality of the goods. I sold clothing of all sorts, mostly to the miners who came to Sacramento to make their purchases, and what success I had was mainly due to an improvement I invented about that time to prevent overalls slitting open (the endless-fly overall I called it). I used to sell a pair of overalls with this improvement, which I patented, for 75 cents, and as the nearest to these in quality were the "riveted" overalls which were sold at a dollar and a quarter and were not nearly so strong, my invention soon came to be in great demand. That was the first hit I made, and it was about time too, for it began to look as if I should have to send down to San Francisco for a dollar to keep me alive.

My system of fixed prices was so novel that it was not accepted without a struggle. I remember one day a great big chap came into the store and bought quite a lot of things, perhaps twenty-five dollars' worth; it was the largest piece of business I had done in one go since I started. When he had done buying and I was wrapping up the goods, he noticed a pocketknife I had on view in a little show-case with a few other things. It was marked, if I remember right, 50 cents, and he wanted me to throw it in with his other purchases. I explained to him that I could not do so, that it was against the principle on which I ran the store; that if I gave him a knife I should presently have to give presents to other people, and that such a course would be inconsistent with an equitable mode of doing business. He still insisted, urging that he had not beat me down a cent on the other goods. I refused; then he said, "All right, you can keep your damned traps," and went for the door. "Very well," I replied and threw the parcels on the shelf, and when he still hung about, wanting to haggle, I told him I would not sell them to him anyhow, that he could just get out and go to hell. That was the rough Arizona talk I gave him. And so my best customer was hustled out. He went right enough; but pretty soon, while I was at lunch, a man came in and bought the goods of my relief boy, who usually came to mind the store when I went out. He bought them for himself, but they went to that big chap, all right.

On the Saturday night following, as I was getting ready to shut up, there was quite a rumble on the board sidewalk;

60

it sounded as though a company of soldiers was marching up. Pretty soon the crowd stopped in front of my store and for a moment I thought there was going to be a fight. "There he is," their leader shouted as he came in, pointing to me; "he's the only honest storekeeper in Sacramento, boys. Whatever he says is so. Let's buy him out." It was the fellow I had refused to dicker with a few days before. And sure enough, by the time they had got through with their purchases, there was not much of my stock left.

Well, the big chap of this story was the foreman of the boiler shops in the works of the Central Pacific Railroad Company, and this adventure was soon noised abroad. It marked the turn of the tide. One customer would bring others, and pretty soon I needed a clerk. When he came I said to him, "Do you lie?" "No," says he. "Well, just remember this; if I catch you lying to any customer of mine, out you go." One day I caught him praising up some goods to a woman, saying they were so and so. "No," said I, "tisn't either; that is poor stuff," right out before him. I wouldn't have anyone in the store who was going to lie about the goods. I wanted it to be known throughout Sacramento as a place for fair dealing.

Olivia Rossetti Agresti, *David Lubin: A Story in Practical Idealism* (Berkeley: University of California Press, 1941)

No Jew Admitted

Saratoga, in New York State, was a famous resort town even in the nineteenth century. Each summer the cream of American society vacationed there. One day in 1877 the Grand Union hotel refused to admit Joseph Seligman and his party. Seligman, a banker and a power in the Republican party, had raised $200 million selling war bonds to finance the Union cause in the Civil War. Still, the press called him "the Jew banker." And now the world's largest hotel had declared it would no longer admit him or any other Jews.

Jews had been kept out of other places before, quietly. Professional societies, private clubs, college fraternities had all barred Jews. Some Americans protested this practice, but far more accepted anti-Semitism and were silent. Colleges began adopting quota systems to limit Jewish students. Help-wanted advertisements stated Only Gentiles Need Apply. Jews could not buy or build homes in many neighborhoods—even in whole towns. Their children could not get into private schools.

Seligman resisted discrimination openly. His public protest made the issue of anti-Semitism front-page news. Others rallied to the fight. In Cincinnati, forty-six of the leading Jewish merchants launched a public boycott against Judge Hilton, the New York merchandiser and owner of the Grand Union hotel.

We, the undersigned merchants of Cincinnati, having noticed with a deep sense of indignation the uncalled-for and unjust discrimination made against the Israelites, as a class, by Judge Hilton, of New York, in excluding them as guests from his hotel at Saratoga, protest against this unwarranted action as a gross outrage upon our rights—as an insult to modern civilization and a stigma upon republican institutions. Considering the unanimous stand taken by the press as the representative of public opinion, we are content, as citizens, to leave our cause, as such, in the hands of the American people. As businessmen, however, we deem it due to our self-respect, and we hereby declare and pledge ourselves henceforth to entertain no business relations whatever with the house of A. T. Stewart & Co., of which Judge Hilton is the acknowledged head.

THE NEW YORK TIMES *of June 19, 1877, reported on the "sensation at Saratoga," when the banker Joseph Seligman was refused admittance by the Grand Union hotel because he was a Jew.*

A SENSATION AT SARATOGA.

June 19, 1877 — N Y Times

NEW RULES FOR THE GRAND UNION.

NO JEWS TO BE ADMITTED—MR. SELIGMAN, THE BANKER, AND HIS FAMILY SENT AWAY—HIS LETTER TO MR. HILTON— GATHERING OF MR. SELIGMAN'S FRIENDS —AN INDIGNATION MEETING TO BE HELD.

On Wednesday last Joseph Seligman, the well-known banker of this City, and member of the syndicate to place the Government loan, visited Saratoga with his wife and family. For 10 years past he has spent the Summer at the Grand Union Hotel. His family entered the parlors, and Mr. Seligman went to the manager to make arrangements for rooms. That gentleman seemed somewhat confused, and said : "Mr. Seligman, I am required to inform you that Mr. Hilton has given instructions that no Israelites shall be permitted in future to stop at this hotel."

Mr. Seligman was so astonished that for some time he could make no reply. Then he said: "Do you mean to tell me that you will not entertain Jewish people?" "That is our orders, Sir," was the reply.

Before leaving the banker asked the reason why Jews were thus persecuted. Said he, "Are they dirty, do they misbehave themselves, or have they refused to pay their bills?"

"Oh, no," replied the manager, "there is no fault to be found in that respect. The reason is simply this: Business at the hotel was not good last season, and we had a large number of Jews here. Mr. Hilton came to the conclusion that Christians did not like their company, and for that reason shunned the hotel. He resolved to run the Union on a different principle this season, and gave us instructions to admit no Jew." Personally he [the manager] was very sorry, inasmuch as Mr. Seligman had patronized the hotel for so many years, but the order was imperative.

Mr. Seligman felt outraged and returned to New

The Pogroms
Were All Around Us

Shmuel Goldman was an immigrant tailor from Poland—then part of the huge Russian empire—who ended his days in California. "The deepest impressions of my life," he told an interviewer, "are where the roots are set." In his old age he goes back in memory to his youthful years in the shtetl, the small town he came from.

Anti-Semitism was an ancient tradition in Russia. Under the Czar Jews were humiliated and hounded by hundreds of restrictions. Military conscription of Jews was especially heavy—boys were drafted into the army for twenty-five years of service. Whatever the Russian people suffered—poverty, hunger, misfortune—was always blamed on the Jews.

The Russian way of "solving the Jewish problem" was to treat this people like the plague. From 1804 the Jews were forced to live as though quarantined, in a confined region called the Pale of Settlement. It was a rigid policy of segregation designed to save the "Holy" Russian people from contamination by the Jews.

When Czar Alexander II was murdered in 1881, the false charge that "the Jews did it" was rumored everywhere. Pogroms—the organized massacre of helpless people—broke out in many places and tens of thousands of Jews were injured or killed.

Shmuel Goldman tells us why his family was among the 3 million Jews who between 1880 and 1924 joined the mass flight from persecution and poverty.

Oh, how often in our dreams, like a bird, we fly back to the place of our birth, to that little Polish town on the Vistula, which would be to you a small speck on the map, maybe even too insignificant for a map. A few thousand people huddled together, hidden in the hills, but with a view in sight of the beautiful river. In this place, the population was nearly equal Poles and Jews. All were poor. There were the poor and the poorer still.

If you walked through the Jewish quarter, you would see small houses, higgledy-piggledy, leaning all over each other. Some had straw roofs; if shingles, some broken. No cobbles on the streets, and you might not even want to call them streets, so narrow and deep-rutted from wagons. Everywhere children, cats, geese, chickens, sometimes a goat, altogether making very strong smells and noises. Always the children were dirty and barefoot, always the dogs were skinny and mean, not Jewish dogs. They came over from Gentile quarters looking for garbage and cats. You would go along this way until you crossed the wooden bridge into the main platz. Here were the women on market day, sitting in the open, or in little wooden stalls if they were well-off. Around the platz, a few Jewish stores, a stable, the pump with a roof and a bench.

Most important, you would see here two buildings, facing each other on opposite sides of the platz, without smiling. There was on one side the Catholic church, enormous, two big towers of bells, and across from it, the synagogue, small but dignified, topped by pagoda-like roofs covered with sheet metal. The church was built with splendor inside and under the sun it was shining like silver, like a sparkle in God's eye. Otherwise it was all wood. The church stands there sternly, the synagogue's historical enemy—those two looked at each other all the day. The church was built with splendor inside and out. Its glittering beauty displayed itself when the great portals opened. The Jewish children were afraid even to look inside.

You see, that church was the biggest thing we ever saw. From everywhere in the town you could see the towers. You could never forget about it. It was such a beautiful

65

building, but when the great bells tolled it meant trouble for us Jews. When we heard that, we children would run home as fast as we could, back into the Jewish streets. On Sundays and Easter, those were the worst times. The processions came out from the church. The peasants were drinking all the day and night, staggering down the road behind those pictures of the saints they carry. Then if they came across a Jewish child or woman, it could be murder. The hatred would pour out.

You see, matters were never simple there. The pogroms were all around us. Then the soldiers on horseback would tear through the town and leave dead Jews behind. One time, we heard the big bell ring out and there was no reason for it. We were so scared we hid in the synagogue. That was probably the worst place to go, but we were small boys. All night we stayed huddling together there and heard terrible noises outside—horses, screams, shouts. We were afraid to light the lamps or stove. In the morning some men came to get us. Someone, it must have been a Pole, had warned the Jews with the bells that the soldiers were coming through. Everyone got away very quickly, hiding in the forest and in neighbors' homes. Who knows what would have happened without the warning? As it is, the soldiers tore up the Jewish streets, broke windows, threw the furniture out. We came out into the sparkling sunshine and the streets were white like a winter. Everywhere were feathers from where those Cossacks cut up our featherbeds. Dead animals also on our streets. From all this you can imagine our emotions when we walked past the great doors of the church. We would hardly throw a glance inside, even though the beauty would draw us like moths.

Barbara Myerhoff, *Number Our Days* (New York: Dutton, 1978)

Hello, Hello,
Here We Are!

There were reasons enough for one out of every three Jews in eastern Europe to emigrate. Hunger and pogroms were the common explanation. But beyond these social forces there were personal motives. And one of them was takhlis, which in Hebrew means an end goal. Takhlis was a unique guiding principle of east European Jewish life. According to it, you did not find meaning or satisfaction in simply living life: you had to achieve something. If you got somewhere in the traditional spheres of learning, status, or financial security, then you had found takhlis. But in the ghetto so many barriers to achievement existed that your hopes for takhlis were small. What way out was there? America—there was the Golden Land! Many of the younger people of eastern Europe looked to America as the place where they could achieve takhlis.

In America, everyone said, you could work your way up, realize your potential, and educate your children to make their mark in the world. The first problem, however, was to get there. It was never easy. It meant leaving family, friends, familiar old places. It meant finding a way to pay for the long journey across a continent and an ocean. It meant mustering the courage to face the new and the strange.

Edith LaZebnik, a Polish Jew, was one of the millions who came to America. Only sixteen at the time, she recalls the long adventure she risked by herself. It began with the illegal crossing of the frontier.

We were eight girls going to Warsaw on the train. The agent brought us to a hotel, stinking from the street from fish, like a barracks where soldiers stay. At night we slept on the floor and the mice bit our feet. Food? We couldn't eat. It was like garbage. Three weeks we suffered before the agent came back. He told us now to go on the train,

A Jewish girl arriving at Ellis Island in 1905. LEWIS W. HINE

but it was far from the city. We had to walk with our heavy bundles almost a whole day until we came to the train. Then it took us away, and it stopped in a little town. The agent said we had to go to a small house far away from the town. Oy, we walked nearly a whole day again. We had to wait till night the next day, sitting on the floor and sleeping, eating only bread and tea. Night came. It was very dark, and we were eighty people and some little children. One woman was going to her husband, with a one-year-old child. When he went to America, she was pregnant.

Finally, after two days, the agent came and led us out in the dark. On the way there were Russian soldiers. The agent paid them not to look at us. We would lie on the grass in a lot of hay, and then the agent would take us from one soldier to the next. We went that way for fifteen miles. We had no more strength and we all dropped to the ground. If they caught us, we would get shot or they would kill the soldiers. So no one said a word. Then it started to rain. Near me was a woman with a child in her arms, crying. A soldier ran quickly to her and told her she had to keep the baby quiet. But the rain got worse and the baby cried harder. The soldier said, "If you don't keep the baby quiet, I'll have to kill you, or else everybody will be killed."

When I heard that, I was like a dead person, and I told her to give me the child. I rocked the baby and sang a nice song. "Shah, shah," I said softly, and the baby fell asleep. Then I told the mother I couldn't carry the baby anymore, I was so tired. So the mother took the baby again, but it cried. The mother covered its mouth to keep it quiet and she prayed, "God, oy, God, don't let my child die." She wrapped up the baby so tight no one could hear if it cried.

Then a river came and we had to cross up to our waists. One soldier saw that I was going to fall, and he took me on his back. I weighed ninety pounds then. I thanked him and he carried me until daylight. When we came out of the river, wet and without strength, and no sleep or food, we were over the border, but we thought we had still more to go.

Then we saw big wagons with a lot of straw, each one with four horses. By every wagon a man was standing, and we were all scared. It rained so hard we couldn't walk. I felt sick and I cried from the cold. All of a sudden two soldiers came onto the road. They laughed at how we were standing, wet and shaking. The agent whispered quickly we should put together *kupkes*, like quarters, and give to them. We did and they went away. Then he told us to get into the wagons. "Now you're in Germany," he said. "Go in good health." Him we never saw again.

We traveled a half-day till we came to a little town where they took us into a big house with one big room for women and children, and a separate one for men. We waited for them to take us by train to Berlin and then to Bremen, where the ship was. Three weeks we waited. I had brought a little bit to eat; my mother had put it in. But it was all gone. One week they didn't give us food. By me was sewn in my coat fifty rubles. When you came to America, you had to show money. That's the way it was then. I was scared to take out some rubles to buy food. After two days without eating, I took out five rubles.

Finally, like we were dead, they took us out of the house and we went by train to Berlin. There, they put one thousand immigrants in a big place with a lot of bunks for sleeping. One man was standing with a whip whirling over his head like you drive cattle. He hurt me with the whip and it got dark in my eyes, and I cried. A young man ran over and hit him in the face and yelled at him, "We are people!" And everybody started to yell, "We are people!"

In Bremen we had to stay two more weeks, till the boat left. I didn't have what to eat. In the bunk near me was a Polish woman. "Come with me and we'll eat together," she said. But I couldn't; I didn't have any more money. I didn't want to write home because if they sent money, it wouldn't come in time. And that's the way we both lay and talked. She told me she was there for five weeks, from Warsaw she came. She said she had some money and that she would buy me every day a bowl soup. That's the way I ate. The Polish woman said when we get to America we would see each other and I would pay her. She couldn't go yet because she had to heal her eyes. I never saw her again.

Finally came the time we should go and we went to the boat. A little boat we took to get to the big boat. *Bremen* they called it. It was in the Russian war with Turkey, a very old ship. It danced on the water like a ballerina. Everybody got sick right away. The bread was so hard we used

70

to throw it in the ocean. We lay in the bottom of the boat and rats jumped over us as we screamed. There was a big storm and the boat was crying like an old woman, oy, in her bones, and everybody was yelling that pretty soon the boat was going to break, and the sailors were running up and down, and water came in through the bottom.

That's the way it was on the ocean for thirty-two days. We arrived in America on Sunday. Everybody was standing on one side of the boat, so they told us we had to move around or the boat would tip over. Like a hand held toward us, America was waving. Everybody was waving back. Hello, hello, here we are.

Edith LaZebnik, *Such a Life* (New York: Morrow, 1978)

A Human Hodgepodge

One of the newcomers who landed in New York at the beginning of the mass immigration from eastern Europe was Abraham Cahan. He was born in 1860 in Lithuania, then under Russian rule. While working as a Jewish teacher, he joined the revolutionary underground, plotting to overthrow czarism. When Alexander II was assassinated in 1881, Cahan escaped arrest and fled to the United States. He lectured in Yiddish to workers, helped found and edited the Jewish socialist daily, the Forward, *and mastered English and wrote articles and novels in his adopted tongue.*

From his book Yekl *comes this sketch of the variety of Jews living on the lower East Side. That one square mile became the America of the east European Jews. For it was to New York City that most of them came, and in New York City that most of them stayed.*

He had to pick and nudge his way through dense swarms of bedrȧggled half-naked humanity; past garbage barrels rearing their overflowing contents in sickening piles, and lining the streets in malicious suggestion of rows of trees; underneath tiers and tiers of fire escapes, barricaded and festooned with mattresses, pillows, and featherbeds not yet gathered in for the night. The pent-in sultry atmosphere was laden with nausea and pierced with a discordant and, as it were, plaintive buzz. Supper had been despatched in a hurry, and the teeming populations of the cyclopic tenement houses were out in full force "for fresh air," as even these people will say in mental quotation marks.

Suffolk Street is in the very thick of the battle for breath. For it lies in the heart of that part of the East Side which has within the last two or three decades become the Ghetto of the American metropolis, and, indeed, the metropolis of the Ghettos of the world. It is one of the most densely populated spots on the face of the earth—a seething human sea fed by streams, streamlets, and rills of immigration flowing from all the Yiddish-speaking centers of Europe.

Street scene on the Lower East Side in 1912. LEWIS W. HINE

Hardly a block but shelters Jews from every nook and corner of Russia, Poland, Galicia, Hungary, Roumania; Lithuanian Jews, Volhynian Jews, south Russian Jews, Bessarabian Jews; Jews crowded out of the "pale of Jewish settlement"; Russified Jews expelled from Moscow, St. Petersburg, Kieff, or Saratoff; Jewish runaways from justice; Jewish refugees from crying political and economical injustice; people torn from a hardgained foothold in life and from deep-rooted attachments by the caprice of intolerance or the wiles of demagoguery; innocent scapegoats of a guilty Government for its outraged populace to misspend its blind fury upon; students shut out of the Russian universities, and come to these shores in quest of learning; artisans, merchants, teachers, rabbis, artists, beggars—all come in search of fortune.

Nor is there a tenement house but harbours in its bosom specimens of all the whimsical metamorphoses wrought upon the children of Israel of the great modern exodus by the vicissitudes of life in this their Promised Land of today. You find there Jews born to plenty, whom the new conditions have delivered up to the clutches of penury; Jews reared in the straits of need, who have here risen to prosperity; good people morally degraded in the struggle for success amid an unwonted environment; moral outcasts lifted from the mire, purified, and imbued with self-respect; educated men and women with their intellectual polish tarnished in the inclement weather of adversity; ignorant sons of toil grown enlightened—in fine, people with all sorts of antecedents, tastes, habits, inclinations, and speaking all sorts of subdialects of the same jargon, thrown pellmell into one social caldron—a human hodgepodge with its component parts changed but not yet fused into one homogeneous whole.

Abraham Cahan, *Yekl* (New York: Appleton, 1896)

Communes
on the Land

The ignorance and poverty of the east European Jews flooding into New York distressed the German Jews. These "outlandish" Yiddish-speaking foreigners would stir up anti-Semitism, they feared. But as the tide of immigration rose, the German Jews began to form organizations to help the newcomers with money, guidance, training, jobs.

They tried to steer some of the immigrants away from New York, into the interior of the country. Among those who welcomed such help were Russian Jewish idealists. They wanted to build agricultural communes to get away from the old, humiliating occupations, to prove that Jews were not only merchants and traders. The simple rural life, lived on socialist principles, was their goal.

There were sixteen attempts after 1881 to build such agricultural colonies. To Louisiana, South Dakota, Kansas, Colorado, New Jersey, Arkansas they went, loaded down with farm animals, tools, and debts. The new utopians soon found that tilling the soil was backbreaking labor, and unrewarding. Only about 3,000 Jewish families tried it. The dream failed; it was against the times. American farmers by the millions were deserting the land to seek a better life in the cities.

In these excerpts from letters, Jewish farmers in New Odessa, Oregon, write of life on a commune a hundred years ago.

A new life begins for us, which enables us to turn in earnest to our spiritual, moral, and physical development. . . . As soon as we assembled, we threw ourselves heart and soul into our work, which in spite of the meager food we received and the generally unfavorable circumstances of our life, was crowned with a measure of success. . . . Our food consisted of bread, potatoes, peas, beans, and a little milk. We suffered greatly from the cold, for we were short of quilts. . . . Nevertheless, we industriously wielded ax, hammer, and saw, and by the end of the month we managed

74

to furnish 125 cords of wood . . . and were thus convinced that we could meet our obligations. But we have no illusions about the efforts we shall have to make. . . . We know that all the sixteen months, which the contract stipulates, we shall have to work hard. At the end of that period we shall have enough money to pay the first instalment on our farm and for the most essential implements. But at that time we shall remain without a steady source of income, and what will happen then? . . .

About a month ago the Frey family arrived. With their arrival a new regimen was established. We undertook the study of mathematics under the instructorship of Frey, and the study of English, under Marusia and Lydia, the wife and sister-in-law of William [Frey], respectively. This is our daily schedule: We work from six o'clock in the morning till half-past eight in the morning. From half-past eight to three quarters of nine we have breakfast. Work is resumed at ten o'clock and continued to four o'clock in the

A print illustrating facets of life in the Jewish agricultural colony founded in Dakota Territory in the 1880s. AMERICAN JEWISH ARCHIVES

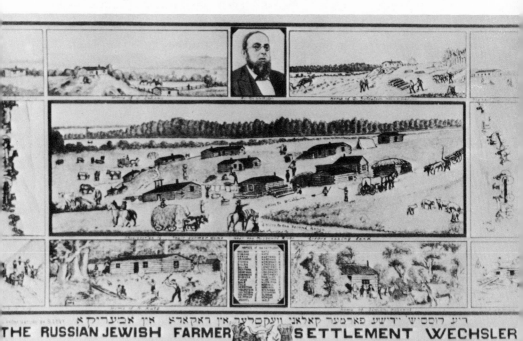

THE RUSSIAN JEWISH FARMER SETTLEMENT WECHSLER
BURLEIGH COUNTY DAKOTA TERRITORY.

afternoon. Between four and five o'clock is dinner, followed by a rest period and intellectual activity. Monday, Tuesday, Thursday, and Friday are devoted to the study of mathematics, English, and to Frey's lecture on the philosophy of positivism. On Wednesday, current matters are discussed and on Saturday, the problems of the "commune." On Sunday we rise at six o'clock and immediately a lively discussion begins on the subject of equal rights for women. In the beginning the women had demanded full equal rights. They had gone to work in the forest, with the men taking their turn in the kitchen and laundry. Soon, however, the women realized that they were not yet fit for that type of work and they returned to their previous tasks. Now they assure us that they have acquired the necessary physical strength and endurance for work in the forest. . . . Thus the time passes till breakfast. This meal consists of rice, oatmeal, baked and raw apples, beans, potatoes, bread and milk. (The members of the "commune" are vegetarians.) After breakfast, one member goes to survey the farm, another reads a newspaper or a book, the rest sing, shout, and dance. At four o'clock dinner is served. Two men wash the dishes, the choir sings, the organ plays. . . . At seven o'clock in the evening begins a session of mutual criticism; then the work for the week is assigned.

Abraham Menes, "The American Oxlam Movement," *YIVO Annual,* Vol. IV, 1949

Sweatshop

The first thing the new immigrant needed on arrival was a job. The German Jews who had come earlier now owned garment factories in lower Manhattan. The Russian Jews found work in those shops and settled nearby. Although a majority entered the needle trades, Jews could be found in many other occupations, for none was barred to them.

In the old country, work done with the hands was looked down upon. In America, however, it was no disgrace to do such labor. A tailor, a plumber, a carpenter was as good as anyone else. But for the 60 percent of the newcomers who ended up in the garment sweatshops, the work was killing.

Harry Roskolenko was only five when he saw his first sweatshop. He came on a visit to bring his father a letter and an apple. His father worked at a pressing machine.

When I arrived at the factory there he was, my father, soaking wet with sweat. It was just an ordinary shop, I discovered, with nothing special about the men, the work, the heat, the dirt, the pay, the boss, the production. It was a factory with a hundred workers stripped down to their pants. All sorts of tailoring, cutting, and pressing machines were whirling, whirring and steaming away. I was fascinated for a few minutes—then I saw my father. I lost the magic of a new place at once. The inventions were gone—and there was a man of fifty, pressing a cloak with a ten-pound steam iron.

It was summer sweat, winter sweat, all sorts of sweat; bitter, sour, stinking, moldy—through all the seasons of the year. Not one fan to blow up some wind. The fans were in the boss's office. Nor were there radios, then, to make things more rhythmical, happier, more energizing. Somebody hummed or whistled. A few pigeons would reach the fire escapes for the bits of stale bread that a worker had put there—for a moment of flight and magic. The pigeons would make off, when the steam blew their way. Instead of fans there were foremen walking about, fuming and blowing, their voices like dogs barking at other dogs.

The workers seldom paused, no matter what they were at. They talked every language but English; and the fore-

A sweat shop in New York's garment district. LEWIS W. HINE

man, when queried over some confusion in the work, answered in every language. When the foreman laughed, everybody laughed—machinelike, blending with the pigeons, the smells, and the steam, into one great bubble of gas. After the laugh—back; the moment gone, allowed, created by some eccentricity on the part of the foreman. It had likely cost the whole factory a dollar in production. And no one smoked except during lunch or when a worker went to the toilet. They were watched there as well. How long does it take to urinate? I heard the foreman say in Yiddish, *"Vi lang nemt es tsu oyspishn? Or tsu kakn? Shnel! Shnel!* Hurry. Hurry—get back to work, *pisher!"*

Yes, how long to urinate, how long to move your bowels? Nothing in nature took very long over piecework or the need to produce downtown what was needed uptown at the end of the day or that afternoon. Nothing but what went on at the tables. . . .

They were producing winter wear, heavy coats and

cloaks, in the summertime. Outside, the temperature was almost 100 degrees. Indoors, it rose to 110 or 120—humid, steamy, all-encasing, gluey. At the tables they got so much per garment pressed or so much for sewing on sleeves, collars, linings, bodies—whatever went to make up the finished garment. It was so little usually and the cause of many strikes and sudden stoppages. With this system of sweating, every worker gave up his lunchtime—the minutes saved, to earn a bit more. Eat faster or eat less. Or eat what took up no time at all—and then back to the steam and the machines, and to the *gontser macher* barking to his dogs.

The day began in the dark, too early for the sun's rising, and it ended in the dark, too late for sun's setting. It was twelve hours, fourteen hours, sixteen, depending on what the worker needed at home. The nature of piecework had its own dictation, or strength, or fears, or all sorts of public and private mathematics and shorthand—to dictate the hours. Yes, what was needed at home? What was not? Who was coming over from Poland, Russia, Hungary—another relative? How much did the *shifskart* [ship's passage] cost? And the money might or might not be paid back. Another pogrom, too . . . and my father had read the letter. . . .

I would see my father rise at five in the morning. . . . He would dress quietly. The children must not be disturbed because of school, because of their studies, because of our future. . . . My mother was heating milk, chickoried coffee, oatmeal—breakfast. Into the coffee went brown sugar. Into the coffee went some cognac—to warm him up. The house was cold; or, when the huge stove was going, like a Turkish bath . . . and we lived between these extremes of cold and heat. And she was packing his lunch—last night's dinner.

My father was off in a hurry. On the way he picked up a Yiddish newspaper, usually the Socialist *Forward.* Once at 110 Greene Street he was in the middle of a mad mob of workers, all trying for the freight elevator. Fire buckets laced the inside of the entrance along with buckets of sand. The factory floors were wooden like the broken stairs. But the freight elevators were for freight, not for the workers— for great bundles of cloaks, bolts of cloth, linings, the guts of the factory. Porters, truckmen, horses, errand boys, and the men of the machines, all were trying to merge their way into the cable-pulled elevator, which had a safety door that slid down when the elevator slid up. But soon the men like my father gave up and were walking up the nine floors, spitting, coughing, cursing, making jokes that no one laughed at—with nine floors upward to go. . . .

Now they were at their machines and pressing tables. They looked even stranger in the dark, with the dangling bulbs lighting up their small places near hell—a gang of prisoners about to break rock. It was, each man soon discovered as he set his watch, 6:00 A.M. The piecework day had begun.

Now my father was at the pressing table, a big rack to his left, with the unpressed cloaks, and one to the right, where the pressed cloaks went—and the rack to the right was the one that counted at the end of the day. So much for so much—the amount I no longer recall. The foreman counted the rack up at noon or at odd hours, when shipments were being readied. My father noted everything down in a little book that he scrawled into during the day; the amount pressed, when pressed, and the name of the boy who took them off the rack. For there was always disagreement regarding the tallies, or the truth, or the lies; and the little pencil my father wetted on his tongue to make the color come out blue was his truth. When they argued, as each man did with his foreman, there was only one truth left—each man's book in his pocket. Often, too, the foreman and the boy were working it out together—a small racket that made one old man somewhat poorer at the end of the week.

My father was, soon enough, a steam engine with his pressing iron. Here, there, top, bottom, lapels, sleeves, back—the coat was pressed, hung, noted—and he reached for another. His small body was like a piece of sculpture caught in some form of motion; an engine puffing; an engine riding into a station; a bursting continuity of steam, thin muscles, sharp reflexes—and cloak went after cloak, done, counted. On and on it went, wearing him to death.

Harry Roskolenko, *The Time That Was Then* (New York: Dial, 1971)

Taking in Boarders

The lower East Side became the most crowded slum in New York City, perhaps in the world. Everyone lived in tenements six or seven stories tall—"great prison-like structures of brick," one reporter described them, "with narrow doors and windows, crowded passages and steep, rickety stairs." They were deathtraps in time of fire. Drainage in the streets was terrible, and the air stank. The apartments were small, three or four rooms, invariably crowded, and lacking all privacy.

To make ends meet, a family often took in boarders—three, four, five, even more—turning the home into a teeming barracks. Yuri Suhl, an immigrant from Poland, writes of a widow who earned her living taking in boarders, converting her kitchen into a restaurant to feed them. His story tells a lot about the people of the lower East Side and their worries.

Mrs. Rosenthal was a widow in her early fifties, who earned her living by running a "private restaurant" in the kitchen

81

Large families on the Lower East Side crowded into single rooms in bleak tenements. The reporter Jacob Riis took this photograph in 1910. THE BETTMANN ARCHIVE, INC.

of her own home. Although the kitchen table could accommodate only six people, there were usually eight or ten boarders crowded around it. And if someone brought an eleventh one along, he was not turned away. Mrs. Rosenthal would add a chair to the table and a cup of water to the soup pot. Her motto was: "If there is enough for ten, there is enough for one more."

Her boarders were all immigrants, most of them her own *landsleit* from Rumania. My father and I were the only Galicians among them.

This made us an easy target for some good-natured kidding. We were known as the *galitzianer,* and every night without fail, when my father and I came for supper, someone at the table would joyfully exclaim, "Mrs. Rosenthal! The *galitzianer* are here already!" To which Mrs. Rosenthal would retort, "And if the *galitzianer,* so what? *Galitzianer* are also people. . . ."

The humorist among the boarders, and by far the most talkative of them, was Shmerl Kalodny, a pants operator. He had small, but gay and vivacious, eyes that gave his tired, middle-aged face a boyish appearance. They called him *der kommediant* (the comedian), and he both cherished and lived up to his title. Whenever he was at the table, the kitchen resounded with laughter. Even Reb Simcheh, a rag assorter, whose serious face was always a blend of gray beard and gray rag dust, would grudgingly crack a smile at Shmerl's jokes.

Shmerl had an enormous appetite, and for each dish he had a separate comment. He would look at the small plate of chopped beef liver, which Mrs. Rosenthal served as an entrée with monotonous regularity, examine it from all sides, and call out, "Mrs. Rosenthal! What are you running, a drugstore or a restaurant?"

"The comedian is talking already," Mrs. Rosenthal would mutter into her pots, with mock annoyance. "Eat, eat, and save the questions for Passover."*

"Until Passover I'll have plenty more questions, Mrs. Rosenthal. Right now, answer me this: Do you measure out your portions with an eye-dropper, or do you weigh them on a pharmacist's scale?"

When it came to the soup—and it was always noodle and *kashe* with a few lima beans thrown in—Shmerl would run his spoon around the plate and exclaim excitedly, "Mrs. Rosenthal! Mrs. Rosenthal! You made a mistake! I should live so, you made a mistake!"

Mrs. Rosenthal would place her hands challengingly on her hips and say, "Whatsematter again already?"

"Yesterday I counted eight noodles and today I got nine. You better take one back. I'm afraid I'll overeat, God forbid, on the extra noodle."

---

* The reference is to the Four Questions which the youngest asks the elder at the Seder on Passover eve.

After supper the boarders would go into the living room, occupy the two upholstered armchairs and the big, battered sofa, and talk. That is how they spent the rest of the evening—smoking and talking. The two favorite subjects of their conversation were news from their families in Europe and the needle-trade market.

With the exception of my father and old Reb Simcheh, both widowers, they were all married men who had left their families behind in Rumania or Poland and had come to America to work and to save enough money to bring their families over. In the meantime, they supported their families by sending home regularly part of their earnings.

Some had changed their plans and had decided to make their "big fortune" here and then go back to Europe. They were disappointed in America. They called it the land of hurry-up that sold its soul to the dollar. Hersh Boimel was one of them. He was a tall, thin, sallow-faced man with high cheekbones and tired eyes. He coughed continuously, and there was talk among the boarders that he had a touch of consumption.

His *landsmanshaft* [hometown group] society doctor had told him to quit the shop, go away to the country for some rest, and then find some open-air occupation like window-cleaning or fruit peddling.

But Hersh had shrugged off the doctor's advice. "It's easy for him to say quit the shop and go to the country. And what will I send my wife and children? Fresh air? Fresh air they have plenty in Rumania." And he continued working in the shop, and during the busy season he worked overtime and Sundays too.

His *landsleit* offered to run a theater benefit for him and send him away to a sanitarium. But he refused the offer. "I didn't come to America to accept charity," he said proudly.

Whenever he was seized by one of his coughing spells

that made him gasp for breath, he would say, "I am in a race with the *malech hamuves* (angel of death). I am running away from him and he is chasing after me. If I manage to hold out till I'm on the boat back to Europe, I'll be all right. I don't think he will chase me all the way across the ocean."

But one day Hersh lost the race. It was a hot afternoon in July. He was brought home in a taxicab by a fellow pants operator whose sewing machine was next to Hersh's.

Mrs. Rosenthal was out shopping at the time. But Hersh, one of her three "regular" boarders who not only ate there but lived there too, had a key of his own. The man wanted to call an ambulance, but Hersh pleaded with him not to.

"I don't want to be with strangers," he said. "I want to be near my own people. This is the only home I have now. Mrs. Rosenthal will take care of me." So the man called Hersh's Society doctor instead, but when the doctor came he found Hersh unconscious. An hour later he died.

Yuri Suhl, *One Foot in America* (New York: Macmillan, 1950)

Landsleit
by the Dozens

From Dubrovna, a village on the banks of Russia's Dnieper River, came the Merlin family, to end up eventually in an American city they had never heard of. The Merlins were weavers of prayer shawls, desperate to escape oppression piled on top of poverty. Two of the younger brothers, Beryl and Michel, were the first to leave home. They crossed Europe and reached London. It took a year at odd jobs for them to

save enough for passage across the Atlantic. In 1906 they landed and
were swallowed up by the garment sweatshops. But within a year a
depression set in, and they lost their jobs. They went to the Industrial
Removal Office, a Jewish social agency that steered thousands of immi-
grants past New York City into smaller cities around the country.
Given train tickets to Atlanta, the Merlins headed for a new world
even stranger than New York.

The two young men started peddling notions in the rural districts
outside Atlanta and with help from others soon managed to set up
two small groceries—"Mom and Pop stores" they were called.

In the sixty years that followed, the eight immigrant Merlins produced
thirty-four children and countless grandchildren. Michel Merlin set
down in Yiddish an account of the family story from which this passage
is translated. It shows how the immigrants helped themselves, forming
groups to provide mutual benefits. Many were fraternal societies,
landsmanschaften made up of Jews who came from the same village in
the old country. Other groups formed around political views. Landsleit
meant family. All Dubrovners were like one.

By 1907 news spread in New York that Beryl and I were
in business in Atlanta. The depression was still on and landsleit from Dubrovna by the dozens began to come down
to Atlanta. Our credit was good—we had our two small
grocery stores—and we could borrow up to a thousand dollars from small banks to pay back in a year. So we used
that credit to buy stores for the Dubrovners, one after another. They all lived sparingly and paid us back the loans.

The newcomers all knew that they could eat and sleep
with us till they could get on their own feet. That's why
so many newcomers to Atlanta became grocers. Let the first
one be a shoemaker and the others become shoemakers.
The same with grocers.

In 1908 we organized the Workmen's Circle Branch 207
(Arbeiter Ring). We enlisted all the newcomers we could
who had been Socialists or Labor Zionists back in Poland

and Russia. Our aim was self-education and assistance to one another.

Back in New York we had already started to save money to buy ship tickets to send back to our family in Dubrovna. We saved in Atlanta, too, and gradually our family came across the ocean to us. Finally we had with us our mother, our sister, and our five other brothers, including Lazear Ari with his wife and four children. We were all happy. The whole family was here. But when the first World War began our mother stopped getting letters from her sister in Dubrovna. She was uneasy. We assured her the war could last only a few months—everyone thought so at the time. But as the months passed she became more worried, and would sit for hours alone in her room, silent. One night she came out of her room and tearfully asked us, "How can it be that they won't let a letter through from a sister? Why don't you get a minyan of ten Jews together and go to the American Czar and ask him how he could allow that sisters cannot keep in touch with each other for such a long time? How can he allow it?" There was such pathos in her question that we felt more pain than we could bear.

By now there were about 100 Dubrovners in Atlanta. We sent money to Dubrovna after the war, each to his own people. Once we sent a very large sum of money through the new Soviet government, to the entire population of Dubrovna, the *goyim* as well as the Jews, so as not to create bad feelings towards the Jews there. Later we learned from a Russian visitor that the government said it knew better who was in need. . . .

All of us are truly happy and lucky that we ran away from Russia and came to the new and free America. America, be blessed for all the good that you gave to us.

American Story: The Merlin Family, Anti-Defamation League of B'nai B'rith, 1982

To Keep You a Jew

Only a minority of Jewish immigrants—but a strong one—was seriously religious. Another minority was as strongly antireligious. Probably most Jews retained the faith of their childhood but leaned more and more to a secular way of life. They went to the synagogue on the high holy days and only now and then the rest of the year. They continued to observe some of the ritual but not all of it, and many sent their children to cheder and Hebrew school for a Jewish education. In the following excerpt, Harry Roskolenko described what cheders were like.

There were *cheders* for all sorts of Jews—Levantine, Sephardie, Ashkenazi, and I was one of those, I was told—an Ashkenazi, a Russian Jew. Our Yiddish and our Hebrew accents set us off from the others; therefore, I had to go to a *cheder* for the Ashkenazi—and I went . . . every afternoon, . . . to spend the hours between 3:30 and 6:00 P.M. at a dismal basement school on East Broadway. There, in some class or another, with kids that I had never seen before, I was soon arguing about all sorts of commentaries and resolving nothing. Yet it was an education to keep you a Jew; to give you pride in an ancient language; to learn codes, ethics, history—and all about the past heroism of my people at another time.

You learned, or you were slapped. No permission from parents was needed for slapping. It was expected, all too proper, and it had been done in Russia, Poland, Hungary— in all the ghettos of Eastern Europe. It went with learning faster, or better—to accomplish what too often could never be done, in New York. The city was too big. Too many other races and nationalities and a heritage that set us apart—that did not melt us into one huge glob of nationhood—were all over New York. You learned what you wanted to learn, by rote, under stress, while asleep, while rushing to the toilet, while rushing back—with only two minutes given you to take care of your natural functions. And back you were at the little table or desk. You were sitting on a harsh bench. A small potbellied stove was behind you—preparing you to become, one day, a mature-enough Jewish male. . . .

Somebody, a *melamed,* was up front. He was either too young or too old. He was not American-born; it was too soon to develop American-born Hebrew teachers. The lesson at the *cheder* was an education on top of another . . . for there were English lessons to be done that evening along with our Hebrew lessons; our public-school studies running together with our *cheder* studies. But galling homework was homework whether in English or in Hebrew.

But there were *cheders* teaching more than *Khumesh* (Pentateuch). There was Zionism-in-the-making, and the Haskalah, or the European Enlightenment Movement. All schools, when not orthodox *cheders,* had other social, political, and religious nuances behind them. There was the Love of Zion Movement, to bring out a future Zionist—for migration to Palestine. There was the Torah and Srorah school—learning and business—which must have had some appeals in New York, especially with the masses of immigrants rag-picking their way off the streets of Manhattan—to learn, to earn, to become a *mentsh,* proper; to be one's own and no longer a waif, awaiting the charity of relatives to begin or to end. There was the school, too, which concluded in the Talmudic stricture—"Respect the stranger but suspect the stranger." And the Jews knew that too intimately. The pogroms were not too far behind. They were strangers themselves—alien in a city of millions; sick, housed in tenements, the water tap in the yard, and the toilets there, too; strangers in a world of woe. They had a strange gift for comedy and it entered their language and their folklore.

We knew, too soon after the rabbis tried to make us good Jews, Yiddish words like *umglik*—tragic; *seykhl*—sense; *bobbe-myseh*—a tall story; *oysgematert*—tired out; *goneyvishe shtiklekh*—tricky doings. Our words were all too well-related to our scholarship. We got the comedy and the tragedy easily mixed. There was *Az okh un vey*—tough luck; *gehakte tsores*—utter misery; *graubyon*—unmannered man; *mis*—ugly; *peygern zol er*—he should drop dead; and *balebatish*—respectable . . . and rarely indeed was such a word thrown at us.

It was like that in Yiddish. In Hebrew all was much more chosen, delicate, revered, holy—and nothing of an insulting nature was ever said to us in Hebrew. Our thoughts dealt with God—and Judaism. Hebrew concerned great tomes, worn away, and we were the children of those tomes. And the *melamed,* the *tsadek in peltz,* the man who was the scholar above all scholars, who wore a fur hat, a fur coat, who arbitrated between comments and commentaries—he was the esteemed judge of our world.

And the old rebbes used to come down our street, worn away by errant boys. And they brought with them the folklore and the ritual . . . and we took of both and became, years later, what we became in the United States.

Roskolenko, *The Time That Was Then*

First Day at School

Mary Antin was thirteen when her father sent for his family in Polotzk to join him in Boston. He had migrated three years earlier to make a start for them in America. The Antins found life hard; one business venture after another failed. Finally they settled in the slums of Boston's

*South End, where it took the combined earnings of father and two
children to keep the family afloat.*

*The first day of school for his children was a hallowed event in
Mr. Antin's life as well as in theirs. Their reverence for education
had ancient roots in the traditional Jewish commitment to scholarship.
The study of the Bible and Talmud was the pathway to God, and
religious scholars had great prestige. Education for all males was therefore
a goal of Jewish society. The more Jewish learning you had, the better
person you would be.*

*In America, many immigrants had their first chance to study Western
thought and culture. Some discarded religious learning altogether and
gave their energy to secular study. The freedom to go to school was
cherished as passionately as the freedom to make a living. The two
became linked as secular education opened the door to success in America.*

*Such success was realized early by young Mary Antin. She turned
out to be an excellent student. Within four months she learned English
well enough to have a composition published in an educational journal.
Her poems were printed in the Boston papers. When she was eighteen,
a book of her Yiddish letters to an uncle remaining in Polotzk was
published in translation. In 1912, her recollections of the immigrant
years,* The Promised Land, *won popular success. In a passage from
this book, she recalls her first day in a Boston school.*

So it was with a heart full of longing and hope that my
father led us to school on that first day. He took long strides
in his eagerness, the rest of us running and hopping to
keep up.

At last the four of us stood around the teacher's desk;
and my father, in his impossible English, gave us over into
her charge, with some broken word of his hopes for us
that his swelling heart could no longer contain. I venture
to say that Miss Nixon was struck by something uncommon
in the group we made, something outside of Semitic features
and the abashed manner of the alien. My little sister was

Mary Antin (Mashke) and her sister Fetchke in a photograph made in Polotzk before her family emigrated to Boston.

as pretty as a doll, with her clear pink-and-white face, short golden curls, and eyes like blue violets when you caught them looking up. My brother might have been a girl, too, with his cherubic contours of face, rich red color, glossy black hair, and fine eyebrows. Whatever secret fears were in his heart, remembering his former teachers, who had taught with the rod, he stood up straight and uncringing before the American teacher, his cap respectfully doffed. Next to him stood a starved-looking girl with eyes ready to pop out, and short dark curls that would not have made much of a wig for a Jewish bride.

All three children carried themselves rather better than the common run of "green" pupils that were brought to Miss Nixon. But the figure that challenged attention to the group was the tall, straight father, with his earnest face and fine forehead, nervous hands eloquent in gesture, and a voice full of feeling. This foreigner, who brought his children to school as if it were an act of consecration, who regarded the teacher of the primer class with reverence, who spoke of visions, like a man inspired, in a common schoolroom, was not like other aliens, who brought their children in dull obedience to the law; was not like the native fathers, who brought their unmanageable boys, glad to be relieved of their care. I think Miss Nixon guessed what my father's best English could not convey. I think she divined that by the simple act of delivering our school certificates to her he took possession of America.

Mary Antin, *The Promised Land* (Boston: Houghton Mifflin, 1912)

A Full Man

When a Jewish boy reaches thirteen he is considered to be entering the age of maturity. He takes part in a religious ceremony of Bar Mitzva at the synagogue. (The ritual is now open to girls, too; the ceremony is called Bas Mitzva.) Charles Angoff, raised in the Jewish quarter of Boston, recalls how he became a man.

I was Bar Mitzva on Thursday.
My father woke me up at 6:30 in the morning and took me to *shul.* There were about thirty people at the service.

I was called to the Torah for the first time—and that was *Bar Mitzva*. Some of the other congregants came over to me and wished me *mazel tov*. My father bashfully put his arm around me and also congratulated me. Then he and I walked a bit and he went off to work. I turned toward home feeling terribly lonely. I had become a full, mature Jew—and most of Boston was asleep, and didn't care. The few people who passed me on the street didn't care either. When I reached our house, as soon as I put my hand on the doorknob, my mother opened the door and threw her arms around me and kissed me and hugged me and kissed me again. Her arm around me, she took me to the kitchen, and there on the table was the *Shabbes* tablecloth. To my mother it was *yom tov*. She had the usual *boolkes* on a platter, but there was also a platter of the kind of cinnamon cakes I liked, and a smaller platter of ginger jam, another favorite of mine. Also a cup of cocoa. "Eat, Shayel, eat," said my mother. I suggested she have some cocoa too. "No, I'm not hungry." I ate. I was conscious that she was looking at me with great appreciation of what had happened to me. Her oldest son was now a full man in Israel. I was embarrassed, but I was also delighted. I finished my cocoa, and mother said, "Have another cup." The last time she had suggested I have another cup of cocoa was when I was convalescing from a cold that had almost turned into pneumonia. I had another cup. When I was finished with my special breakfast, mother said, "Father had to go to work. He had to. You understand."

"Sure," I said.

"But we'll have a small reception on Saturday night, after *mincha*. We've invited the relatives and some friends. So we'll have a little reception."

"Oh," I said, too moved to say anything else.

She got up, came to me, patted my head and then kissed me slowly. "Maybe you're a little sleepy, Shayel. Maybe you want to sleep a little more. I'll wake you up in time for your school."

"Yes, I think I'll have a little more sleep," I said.

I didn't want any more sleep. I lay down on the bed. I was profoundly happy. Everything was good. Everything was very good.

Charles Angoff, *When I Was a Boy in Boston* (Boston: Beechhurst, 1947)

Neighborhood Nurse

When Lillian Wald was twenty-five, she got her first look at life in the slums of the lower East Side—mounds of garbage rotting at the curb; families crowded into airless rooms, sleeping on rags and boards; crumbling fire escapes; mold, sickness, death. She had grown up in a comfortable German Jewish home in Rochester, New York. Her family gave liberally to the poor, but at a safe distance. On that day in 1893, she had been called out of her medical classroom to tend a sick woman in a tenement. The experience challenged her to leave medical school and begin a lifework as a public health nurse.

Soon she opened a pioneering settlement house on Henry Street, introducing the concept of public health nursing to America and the world. When her immigrant neighbors founded trade unions, she supported their efforts. She was in the forefront of the child welfare movement. She built bridges between the German and the east European Jews, getting them to work together for social reforms.

In letters she wrote to the banker Jacob Schiff, who helped finance her work, she reported what she saw and what she did.

Visit and care of typhoid patient, 182 Ludlow Street. Visit to 7 Hester Street where in rooms of Nathan S. found two

Lillian Wald as a student nurse at New York Hospital.

children with measles. After much argument succeeded in bathing these two patients and the sick baby. The first time in their experience. They insisted no water and soap could be applied to anyone with measles for seven days.

Gave tickets for Hebrew Sanitarium excursion to Mrs. Davis and three children, Mrs. Schneider and five children for Tuesday's excursion, but five of the seven children are nearly naked, and, I am convinced, have no apparel in their possession. So we will make their decent appearance possible for the picnic.

Many of these people have kept from begging and it is not uncommon to meet families, to whom not a dollar has come in in seven months—the pawn shop tickets telling the progress of their fall, beginning some months back with the pawning of a gold watch, ending with the woman's waist.

The multitude of unemployed grows and many who had been able to live [without work] for the first few months are now at the end of their resources. However we are glad in one respect, that having no money to engage the midwife they allow us to furnish doctors . . . who do intelligent, good work.

In a rear tenement, top floor, on Allen Street, a doctor found a woman, a Mrs. Weichert, crazy and ill with pneumonia and typhoid; cared for by her fourteen-year-old daughter. She had been crazy for some time and the husband and child had kept it secret, fearing she would be forcibly taken to an asylum were it known. Though she died in a few days, I shall always be glad that one doctor told us in time so that she was made human and decent, bedding given, and the child assisted to making her dwelling fit for habitation before her end.

Lily Klein very ill with pneumonia, for whom we procured medical attention and nursed. The child died, but the night before Miss Brewster had remained with the child all night. She was ineligible for hospital as she had whooping cough. Father deserted and mother worn out, was not safe to leave a child so ill with.

Annie P., 44 Allen Street, front tenement, second floor. Husband Louis P. came here three years ago and one year ago sent for wife and three children. From that time, unfortunately, his trade, that of shoemaker, became less remunerative. She helped by washing and like labor, but two months ago he deserted her, though she stoutly maintains he returned to Odessa to get his old work back. The youngest, Mayer P., age five years, fell from the table and injured his hip. He lay for 7 months in the Orthopedic Hospital, 42nd Street; he was discharged as incurable and supplied with a brace. . . . The mother is absolutely tied by her pregnant condition; the cripple is in pain and cries to be carried. They had no rooms of their own but paid $3 a month to Hannah A., a decent tailoress, who allowed the family to sleep on her floor. . . . Sunday I saw them. Monday I filed application with Montefiore Home for Mayer's admission. . . . Tuesday I went to Hebrew Sheltering Guardian Society, saw Superintendent, and obtained promise of place for the two well children by Thursday. . . . Thursday afternoon we washed and dressed the two children, and I left them in the afternoon at the Asylum, leaving my address for the Superintendent so that he might know their friend in case of need. They have absolutely no one in America but their mother.

Lillian Wald Papers, Rare Books and Manuscripts Division, The New York Public Library, Astor, Lenox and Tilden Foundations

A Sunday in the Park

Summer in the East Side tenements and sweatshops was like a season in hell. The children found temporary relief splashing in the fountains of public squares or swimming in the East River. The flat roofs of the tenements were turned into playgrounds, the asphalt streets into ball fields. In the evenings the neighborhood candy store became the social center. For those who could afford it, a week or two in the Catskills, where farmers turned their modest homes into summer boardinghouses, was best of all. Soon enterprising Jewish families bought farmhouses and land and developed flourishing vacation resorts.

For the working poor and their children an excursion uptown into Bronx Park was a great holiday. Michael Gold captures the flavor of one such Sunday in the park.

At last the Bronx Park! My father bought us popcorn to eat, and red balloons. Then we walked through some green fields. My mother sighed as she sniffed the fragrant air.

"Ach," said my happy mother, "it's like Hungary! There is much room, and the sky is so big and blue! One can breathe here!"

So we walked until we came to a menagerie. Here we saw a gang of crazy monkeys in a cage. They were playing tag. We fed them peanuts and watched them crack open the shells. Then we saw a lion, two tigers, a white bear, some snakes, birds, and an elephant. All of them we gave peanuts.

Then we walked far into a big lonesome country. It had a big field with no one in it. It had a forest at one end. We looked for signs: KEEP OFF THE GRASS. There were no signs. So we walked into the middle of the field, and found a wonderful tree. This tree we made our own.

We spread newspapers under the tree, and my mother laid out the lunch. We were hungry after our long ride and walk. So we ate the salami sandwiches and other good things.

My father drank two bottles of beer. Then he stretched on his back, smoked his pipe, and looked at the sky. He sang Roumanian shepherd songs. Then he fell asleep, and snored.

My mother cleaned away the newspapers. Then she

looked to see if no policeman was near. There was no policeman. So she took off her shoes and stockings and walked around on the grass.

My sister and I left her and went hunting for daisies. We found some and brought them to her. She wove for us two daisy crowns out of them, the sort children wear in Hungary.

Then my mother took our hands. "Come," she said, in a whisper, "while poppa sleeps we will go into the forest and hunt mushrooms."

My father heard the whisper. His snores abruptly ended.

"Don't get lost," he mumbled, not opening his sleepy eyes.

"Pooh," said my mother, "lost in a forest? Me?"

"All right," said my father, turning on his side and snoring again.

In the forest everything suddenly became cool and green. It was like going into a mysterious house. The trees were like walls, their leaves made a ceiling. Clear, sweet voices sang through the house. These were the birds. The birds lived in the house. Little ants and beetles ran about under our feet. They lived on the floor of the house.

I smelled queer, garlicky smells. I saw a large gold coin lying in a bed of green. I looked closer, and knew I was fooled. It was sunlight. The sun made other golden lines and circles. I heard running water.

My mother walked in front of us. Her face looked younger. She stopped mysteriously every few minutes, and sniffed the air.

"I am smelling out the mushrooms," she explained. "I know how to do that. I learned it in Hungary. Each mushroom has its own smell. The best ones grow under oak trees."

"I want to pick some," said Esther.

"No!" said my mother, sharply, "you must never do that.

You are an American child, and don't know about these things. Some mushrooms are poison! They will kill you! Never pick them!"

"Do they come on strings?" I asked.

"Those are the grocery store mushrooms," explained my mother. "Ach, America, the thief, where children only see dry, dead mushrooms in grocery stores! Wait, I will show you!"

There was a flush of excitement on her black, gypsy face. We were surprised at our mother. She was always so slow-moving and careful. Now she jumped over big rocks and puddles and laughed like a girl.

"Stop! I think there are mushrooms under those leaves!" she said. "Let me scratch a little and find out. Yes, yes! do you see? My nose is still sharp after all these years! What a pretty silver cap it has! It is a birch mushroom. Its parents are those birch trees. When mushrooms grow near pine trees they are green, and taste of pine. But the oak mushroom is the finest of all. It is a beautiful brown."

She broke off pieces of the mushroom for us to nibble. "It is better with salt," she said. "But how good it is! It is not like the rubbish they grow here in cellars! No, the American mushrooms have no worth. They taste and look like paper. A real mushroom should taste of its own earth or tree. In Hungary we know that!"

We followed her, as she poked around under the trees and bushes for her beloved mushrooms. She found many, and lifted her skirt to make a bag for them. Each new mushroom reminded her of Hungary and of things she had never told us. She talked in a low, caressing voice. She stooped to the mushrooms, and her eyes shone like a child's.

"Ach, how people love the mushrooms in Hungary! In the season every one is in the forest with a big basket to hunt. We had our own favorite spots where we went year after year. We never plucked mushrooms, but cut them

101

close to the roots, like this. It means they will grow again next year. Two other Jewish girls and I always went hunting together."

"Momma, can mushrooms talk to each other?"

"Some people say so. Some people say that at night mushrooms not only talk, but dance with each other. They turn into jolly old men with beards. In the morning they become mushrooms again.

"Birds talk to each other, too, people say. I used to know the names of all the birds, and their songs. I knew good snakes and bad, and killed the bad ones with a stick. I knew where to find blueberries and huckleberries. I could walk twenty miles in a forest and find my way back. Once, two girls and I were lost in a forest for days and found our way back. Ach, what fun there was in Hungary!"

Suddenly my mother flung her arms around each of us, and kissed Esther and me.

"Ach, Gott!" she said, "I'm so happy in a forest! You American children don't know what it means! I am happy!"

Michael Gold, *Jews without Money* (New York: Liveright, 1930)

Magnificently True

Nothing shocked the east European immigrants more than the fantastic material abundance they discovered in America. Some had heard it was the land of plenty, but they could not imagine how plentiful. Others who knew little of what lay ahead found the opulence of America overwhelming. The contrast made the poverty of the shtetl—the small towns or villages where east European Jews lived—seem all the more intense.

Maurice Hindus, fresh from rural Russia at the age of fourteen,

True also were the stories of white bread. At first I could not eat enough of it—sweet rolls, plain rolls, with cinnamon and poppy seeds, without cinnamon and poppy seeds; I ate them during meals and between meals. In walking the streets and seeing displays in bakeries or on pushcarts I often yielded to the temptation of indulging the appetite for them. Yet soon enough, as in the case of fat meat, I tired of white bread. Often I wished I could drop in on Boris the Cattle, as poor a man as there was in the village, ask him to cut me a slab of black bread, retire to a corner beside his huge brick oven and make a meal of it with a cucumber or with nothing more than garlic rubbed on the crusted part. Baked with grated potato instead of with yeast, which the village had not yet discovered, and never fresh except on the day it came out of the oven, its very solidity and coarseness gave it a tang and a relish which the puffy and overrefined American bread never had. I was amazed at my sudden hunger for the black bread of the old days.

Magnificently true were the stories of handkerchiefs and shoes. Here even I had to have a handkerchief, and not only on the Sabbath and on holidays but on weekdays. The sleeve of the blouse or the bare hand might do well enough in the old village, but not in the streets or anywhere else in New York. A woman just could not stoop down and reach for the bottom of her dress, as she might do in the old village, every time she wanted to blow her nose. Nor did girls need to wait for marriage to flaunt a handkerchief before neighbors and make them aware of the good fortune that had come to them. A handkerchief was neither luxury nor adornment, nor badge of superiority, and one needed to be neither landlord nor merchant to be supplied with one at all times and for all emergencies.

And of course nobody walked barefooted nor in *lapti*—not even children, not in the street, anyway; nor did anybody clump about in thick-leathered knee-high boots; and, whatever the shoes that a man wore, he never bothered to soil his hands, the floor, his clothes, by applying grease to them and then wait for hours or overnight for it to soak into the leather and dry before again stepping into them. He got "a shine" while sitting in a comfortable chair, and when he descended to the sidewalk and looked at his shoes, his heart thumped with joy, for they gleamed like mirrors, and no one in the old home, neither the landlord nor the lumberman nor any of the officials in swanky uniforms, ever could make their boots glisten so brilliantly. Most true was the story of cigarette paper, too true. Nobody used wrapping paper, copybook paper, newspaper, for the rolling of cigarettes and, what was more, hardly anybody made his own, anyway. A man bought his cigarettes ready-made and in pretty boxes. Back home neither the landlord's sons nor daughters, when they went riding horseback and smoked, displayed such cigarettes or such pretty boxes.

Shockingly false, of course, was the story of the colors of American pants. True, people did not make them of white homespun or factory-woven linen, nor did they in their choice of fabrics compete for color with buttercups, cornflowers, lilacs, as did our village landlords and their children in the trousers they sported when they went riding horseback. The dark gray of the home-woven woolen cloth, were it not so hot and heavy, would have won complete approval in America. Indeed, instead of talking so much about bright-colored pants, our folk in the old village might better have learned something of the glories of American underwear. Here was something to stir anyone's fancy. The mere contact of the garment with the body gave a man a feeling of gallantry. He could spread his legs, twist his limbs, crawl, climb, jump over beds, chairs, stand on his head, roll on the floor, and yet when he dashed before a mirror to look at himself the suit clung to him as trim and tight as the skin of an apple. Their ignorance of underwear would have made the story all the more exciting to the folk in the old home. . . .

Our people might likewise have heard a few words of the soda fountains that gleamed majestically out of the open stalls and in the candy shops and spouted the palate-pricking carbonated water into a large glass at a price no higher than that of a bar of chocolate on the pushcarts, or at twice that amount when seasoned with a lavish portion of rich and fragrant syrup. And why hadn't anyone ever mentioned the decorative and juice-soaked tomato? Not even the German landlord had yet begun to cultivate it, though it would have made a fit companion to the cucumber, because it could be eaten with bread and potato, made into soup and pickle, served with meat and herring, used as an appetizer after a gulp of vodka, munched as a delicacy in between meals and a special boon for the numerous fast days when neither milk nor meat foods nor eggs were permitted. It might even vie with the cucumber in its appeal to girls at a dance or any other gathering.

Had any of my old neighbors followed me around on my rambles in the streets and peered as I did into the shop windows, they would have been as excited as I was and as bewildered by the arrays of foods in cans, in boxes, in jars, in bottles, in packages, in bags, and by the ornate displays of footwear, clothes, haberdashery, hardware, musical instruments and a multitude of other commodities, of the names and uses of which they might have been as ignorant as I was. They would have been as mystified too by the variety and multitude of tastes and appetites that man had acquired in this thunderous America, so many indeed that they would have wondered how people found the time to indulge the one or the other or even to think of them.

Maurice Hindus, *Green Worlds* (New York: Doubleday, 1938)

Americanized in Record Time

As the immigrants poured in, they were urged to assimilate quickly. The goal of the public schools was to Americanize the newcomers. But in what way? The message was that if you wanted to make it here, you must become "real" Americans. Drop what made you different, forget where your parents came from and what they had brought with them—their language, their culture, their beliefs, their values.

The popular myth was that America was a melting pot of different peoples. Each ethnic group arriving on these shores would lose its identity and take on the cultural characteristics of white Anglo-Saxon Protestants. And this uniformity, this sameness, this conformity to one model was prized as a great achievement.

But among the immigrants were many who resented the pressure to be totally assimilated. They believed democracy granted them the freedom to choose, to be what they *wanted to be, to be* themselves, *not some feeble imitation of anyone else. To abandon their own cultural traditions in order to become 100 percent Americans was a price they did not want to pay.*

Charles Angoff, Russian-born, came to live in Boston in the early 1900s. Later he became a novelist, critic, and editor. In his autobiography he recalls his childhood years and compares his family's slow adjustment to a new life with the way their neighbors—the Greenbergs—Americanized themselves.

They were the precise opposite of us. They became Americanized in record time. Less than six months after they arrived in this country, they served ice cream at dinner or supper every Sunday, and they were the first, in the family at large, to wear low shoes (they were called Oxfords then), the first to spice their food with ketchup, the first to go to the movies more or less regularly and the first to eat such strange vegetables as celery and lettuce.

My father looked upon ice cream as on the whole a shameful thing, and as children's food at best. Whenever he'd see any of his children eat it—and we did manage to get a cone of strawberry or vanilla or chocolate ice cream every now and then, largely through the connivance of our mother—he'd look at one condescendingly and say, "A strange place, America, a very strange place!" As for low shoes, they simply made no sense to him. He couldn't understand anybody wearing them. "Don't they fall off?" he once asked a neighbor who had been here for about ten years. All of us boys wore high shoes till we began to earn our own money. My father never gave in. As for ketchup, he was sure it wasn't kosher, no matter how many rabbis' signatures were on the bottle, and he considered it as fit only for pigs, anyway. "I wouldn't wish it upon the worst Russian hooligan," he said.

The movies he didn't care for at all. During his first five years in this country, he went only once to a silent movie, and then only to please my mother and us kids. When we left the movie house—the picture was *Orphans of the Storm* with the Gish Sisters—he spat on the sidewalk, turned to my mother and, with stern face, said, "There's no telling where next you'll want me to go. I won't do it, I'm telling you that now!"

My mother merely said, "Not so loud. Be quiet." After that, she took us to the movies by herself. But for years he argued with her about it. He sensed something immoral in the whole art of motion pictures and even something atheistical, though he never made these charges openly. That would have reflected upon his family.

In respect to celery and lettuce, he was far more firm. For years he wouldn't allow them in the house. "This is a house for human beings," he said, "not for cows and animals that eat anything that grows. Pooh!"

The Greenbergs had no such troubles with Kivve Greenberg. He took to everything American like the proverbial duck to water. He was a distant cousin of ours, and my father often said that Kivve—he was always referred to at home by his first name, as was his wife, Gooshe—was strange even in Russia. "When he should have been at synagogue studying the Talmud, Kivve was watching the fair in the town square. Just like he eats ice cream now and wears those funny shoes that aren't shoes at all." As time went on Kivve did even stranger things. He went once a week to a public shower bath, where for two cents he got a towel and a piece of soap, and had hot and cold water sprinkled all over him. My father thought that was plain crazy. A bath to him meant a bath—a lot of water in one place, that you could spash and see all around you; not this running, sprinkling water of the showers. Kivve insisted that it was healthy, to which my father said, "In America, being crazy is healthy, it seems."

When Kivve took his three boys to Boston Common to watch a baseball game, my father was so flabbergasted that words failed him. He merely looked at Kivve long and silently, as if to say, "May the good Lord have mercy upon you for degrading yourself and your family so." My father's attitude here was rather complex. He knew I watched a baseball game once in a while, but that didn't bother him. He apparently thought that I would outgrow it when I reached the ripe age of, say, thirteen, or fourteen. But he thought it was not right for a father to aid and abet his children in the baseball foolishness.

Angoff, *When I Was a Boy in Boston*

The Simchat Torah Union

In America, it was said, you could go from rags to riches. No immigrant would become as rich as Rockefeller, but wasn't there room below the top? The newcomers pitched headlong into the fierce struggle to make it. For countless thousands, however, working life would begin and end in a garment sweatshop—where conditions were "revolting to humanity and decency," as a congressional investigation concluded in 1893. A presser putting in 60 hours a week made $500 a year. (At that time $800 a year was the minimum required for a decent life.) Women worked 108 hours a week for $3 to $6.

By 1900 about 200,000 Jewish immigrants and their children were in the garment trade. When they entered it, labor had no rights. But unions among the Jews were soon organized, starting with the United Hebrew Trades. Bernard Weinstein, an organizer, tells of a visit he made to a Jewish union of elderly men.

Among the unions we had at the end of the nineties a few were composed of old men, like the pressers', the butchers', the ragpickers' locals. One of these that we of the United Hebrew Trades helped organize in 1894 was a union of cleaners. Its members, who had mostly been tailors in Europe, operated out of cellars and worked by hand. They'd

RULES FOR PICKETS

Don't walk in groups of more than two or three

Don't stand in front of the shop; Walk up and down the block.

Don't stop the person you wish to talk to; Walk alongside of him.

Don't get excited and shout when you are talking

Don't put your hand on the person you are speaking to. Don't touch his sleeve or button. This may be construed as a "technical assault"

Don't call any one "scab" or use abusive language of any kind.

Plead, persuade, appeal, but do not threaten.

If a policeman arrest you and you are sure that you have committed no offence, take down his number and give it to your union officers.

רולס פיר פיקעטס

געהט נים מעהר ווי 2 אדער 3 אין אין גרופפע

סטעהט נים ביו בהיר פֿו שאפ, געהט אים הן אין אין צירּיק אויף דער בלאָק.

באאפם נים דיא פֿערזאן מיט ־וועלכע איהר וויללט רייזָן, געהט ב־א זיין זיים אין יעדם זים אדהם.

יערם נים עקסימער, יערם נים היך שרייט נים.

לייגם נים איין אייער האנד אויף דער פֿערזאן סם ־וועלכער איהר ־עדם, צוהם אדהם נים כין אירבעל אדער קאום באמם׳אן, געוועצליך קען נים שייו דייסזן או איהר האם אדהם אנגערופֿען.

ר־פּם קיינעם נים "סקעב" נעברויכם נים קיין בעלייָדיגענדע שפּ׳אך

בעם אין רייזָם אימער צו ־ייָען דיא פֿערזאן מעהר נים, סטרא שעם נים

א־ג קען איעעסטירם אייך און איהר זייָ־םט אז איהר וים אנשיל־די פֿערשרייָבם יעם פּאליסמאנס נומבעָ־, איהר קענם אדהם נאכהעָ־ פֿערק׳אגען.

CIRCULAR ISSUED BY THE STRIKERS.

A leaflet issued by striking workers in New York's garment center.

take dirty old clothes, wash them with benzene, dye them with brushes, and then press them. Many a time their pails of kerosene would spill over and cause fires in the tenements.

110

The union of these elderly cleaners had been started by one of its younger members, M. Segal, of the Socialist Labor party, and their meetings turned out to be quite lively—they usually arranged to have representatives of the United Hebrew Trades in order to settle the frequent fights that would break out, fights of joy.

We couldn't really complain about this uncomradely mode of behavior since the worklife of these people was very bitter—old men, usually in yarmulkes, standing twelve to fifteen hours a day by long tables in dirty cellars, cleaning dirty clothes.

One day three of us from the United Hebrew Trades were invited to a meeting held on the top floor of a loft at 49 Henry Street. This time, it turned out, there'd be no fighting—apparently our presence shamed them out of it.

When we arrived, everyone was sitting around a table facing the chairman; all wore yarmulkes except a few younger members with hats. Most were dressed in long smocks resembling caftans. Everyone had a glass of beer in hand, and before him a plate of herring and chunks of pumpernickel.

The place was half dark from the smoke of pipes and one could have been deafened by the banging of the beer glasses. A few fellows served as waiters and would steadily put down glasses of beer with a *"l'chaim."*

The chairman stood on a platform in the middle of the room. When he noticed us—we hadn't known where to sit among the hundred or so members—he summoned us to the head of the table. As we drew near, everyone rose and as the chairman recited our "pedigree" we were resoundingly toasted with the clinking of glasses. . . .

The noise grew. Someone began a Simchat Torah [the Rejoicing with the Torah, a festival celebrated with feasting and merrymaking] melody; glasses continually refilled from a nearby barrel; also, pails of ice to keep the beer cold.

Finally I asked my bearded neighbor; "What's the occasion?"

"How should I know?" he answered. "Every meeting is like this, or else we wouldn't show up. The men give a few dimes apiece, and we have a Simchat Torah. That's how we are—sometimes we kiss each other from happiness, sometimes we fight."

At the end of each of our speeches, we all cried out, "Long live the union!" as the old Jews applauded and bumped glasses. Meanwhile a few started to move aside the tables and began dancing to a Hasidic tune.

In our report to the UHT, we called this group the Simchat Torah Union.

Bernard Weinstein, *Jewish Unions in America*, 1929

The Triangle Fire

In 1910 a long strike of 60,000 cloak makers in New York ended in an agreement for better wages, hours, and working conditions. The Great Revolt, as it was called, established the principle of collective bargaining. It woke the public to immigrant labor's struggle for justice. Not long after, in March of 1911, the Triangle shirtwaist building, the city's biggest factory, where 850 people worked, burst into flames. The workers could not force their way through the locked and heavy iron doors or down the lone fire escape ladder. The elevators went swiftly out of commission. Men and women were burned or smothered to death by fire and smoke, or killed when they plunged from windows to the street far below. In the disaster, 146 workers died, most of them young women.

112

During the mass funeral for the victims, 50,000 people marched silently through the rain in remembrance of the dead. At a meeting to protest the inhuman working conditions that led to such tragedy, Rose Schneiderman, leader of an earlier strike at Triangle, spoke through her tears.

. . . I would be a traitor to those poor burned bodies if I were to come here to talk good fellowship. We have tried you good people of the public—and we have found you wanting.

The old Inquisition had its rack and its thumbscrews and its instruments of torture with iron teeth. We know what these things are today: the iron teeth are our necessities, the thumbscrews are the high-powered and swift machinery close to which we must work, and the rack is here in the firetrap structures that will destroy us the minute they catch fire.

This is not the first time girls have been burned alive in this city. Every week I must learn of the untimely death of one of my sister workers. Every year thousands of us are maimed. The life of men and women is so cheap and property is so sacred! There are so many of us for one job, it matters little if 140-odd are burned to death.

We have tried you, citizens! We are trying you now and you have a couple of dollars for the sorrowing mothers and brothers and sisters by way of a charity gift. But every time the workers come out in the only way they know to protest against conditions which are unbearable, the strong hand of the law is allowed to press down heavily upon us.

Public officials have only words of warning for us—warning that we must be intensely orderly and must be intensely peaceable, and they have the workhouse just back of all

A corner of the Triangle shirtwaist factory immediately after the fire of 1911 that took the lives of 146 workers. BROWN BROTHERS

their warnings. The strong hand of the law beats us back when we rise—back into the conditions that make life unbearable.

I can't talk fellowship to you who are gathered here. Too much blood has been spilled. I know from experience it is up to the working people to save themselves. And the only way is through a strong working-class movement.

Leon Stein, *The Triangle Fire* (Philadelphia and New York: Lippincott, 1962)

On the front page of the Jewish Daily Forward *appeared a dirge by the sweatshop poet Morris Rosenfeld, from which these lines are taken:*

> Over whom shall we weep first?
> Over the burned ones?
> Over those beyond recognition?
> Over those who have been crippled?
> Or driven senseless?

114

Or smashed?
I weep for them all.

Now let us light the holy candles
And mark the sorrow
Of Jewish masses in darkness and poverty.
This is our funeral,
These our graves,
Our children. . . .

Morris Rosenfeld, *Songs from the Ghetto* (New York: Maynard, 1900)

Picketing the White House

When she was twenty-one, Ernestine Hara Kettler picketed in front of the White House and was sent to jail for thirty days. Her crime? Demonstrating for women's right to vote. The year was 1917. Millions of women felt that the ballot belonged to them as much as to men. In a few states, women had already won the right to vote. But the suffragists feared that state by state the battle might take forever. So they launched a militant campaign for an amendment to the Constitution.

The women paraded by the thousands in Washington to show the new president, Woodrow Wilson, and Congress that they would not be denied the ballot. Mobs attacked them, and troops had to come to their aid. When the United States entered World War I in April, 1917, the National Woman's party, which led the suffrage campaign, spoke out against the war. Women picketed the White House with banners reminding Wilson that Democracy Should Begin at Home.

It was in the fall of 1917 that Ernestine had joined the ranks of the picketing suffragists. Born in Roumania of Jewish parents, she emi-grated to New York in 1907. Her father had died, and her mother, an anarchist, tried to support her four children by working in a sweatshop. Like her mother, Ernestine was radical in her ideas. When she finished high school, she took odd jobs, tried to write, and hung around with Greenwich Village artists and feminists. Hearing of the pickets at the White House, she volunteered to join them.

It wasn't just an adventure. As a radical, I believed in justice. It was very just for women to vote and it was highly un-democratic and an outrage that so much opposition had been placed against their getting the ballot. There were, after all, as many women in the country as men. What is this business? Is a woman so far below a man intellectually that she's not fit to vote? When I think of it, it's just incredi-ble! I can't believe it! I condemned it. I was actually outraged that women didn't have the vote! That's why I went down to Washington, D.C.

I don't know how I got there. I didn't have money, so someone must have paid my fare down there. . . . All I remember is that I found myself in Washington, and that I was met at the station and taken to the headquarters of the National Woman's Party. . . .

What they were doing was picketing in groups of four. Each group had a shift. As soon as one group was arrested, then they sent out another group of four. There was a con-tinuous picket line. That's what drove the policemen crazy—they saw no end to the number of women who were picketing!

I met the other three women in my group at the headquar-ters. One of them was Peggy Johns from New York. An-other, whose name I do not remember, was an organizer in the needle trades in New York. The fourth was a lawyer from one of the Western states, either Wyoming or Arizona.

116

They were all between twenty-five and thirty-five. I was the youngest in the group, twenty-one.

We started picketing the second or third day I was there. We walked back and forth, right in front of the White House gates. We had a banner, but I don't remember whether we each carried one banner or whether the four of us carried one long one with four posts on it. There must have been a saying on it. You can't just have a plain banner without something on it to draw attention of the people passing by.

A pretty big crowd would gather every day—at least it seemed pretty big to me. There were always men and women standing there harassing us and throwing some pretty bad insults—and pretty obscene ones. The women weren't obscene, but the men were. Our instructions were to pay absolutely no attention to them. I ignored them. I was brave. My goodness, I was fighting for a cause.

We had some support, but they took their lives in their hands. If any of the bystanders supported us, they could be beaten by the rest of the crowd. Towards the end, they started throwing stuff at the women. In fact, during this period somebody fired a shot through the windows of the Little White House, [our] headquarters. Any woman that happened to be in the right position for it could have been killed. And we couldn't get police protection. We just couldn't get it. The only protection we had was when we were arrested. Then we were protected!

On one of the picketing days, the police hauled us in and took us to jail. All four of us. Immediately the lawyer or somebody was sent to the city jail to bail us out, so we were in jail only about an hour or so. We didn't have to wait too many days for our trial. After all, the National Woman's Party had to board us, and that costs money.

At the trial we all made statements that we were not obstructing traffic, but that the traffic was obstructing us—

which was true. Obstructing traffic and loitering were the charges. We weren't doing either one of them. We were marching. "There were only four of us," we told them, "so we couldn't possibly obstruct traffic. We were on the sidewalk, there was only one row of us, only four of us. There was plenty of room. But unfortunately, a lot of people stopped and they obstructed traffic. None of them were arrested, except us." We were very bold.

The judge asked how old I was, and when I said twenty-one, he was so mad. He scowled. He couldn't believe it. But he had to believe it because he knew that the suffrage party was insistent about that; we had to be twenty-one or over, otherwise we couldn't march.

So we were given thirty days. Before then, only the hard-core criminals like Alice Paul had been given thirty days. After we were sentenced, we were taken to the city jail. That's where we cooked up our political prisoner demands: We were political prisoners. We were not guilty of obstructing traffic. We were not guilty of the sentence as charged. Therefore, we did not owe any kind of work in the workhouse. That workhouse in Occoquan, Virginia, was a real workhouse—you worked or else.

The next morning we were taken in a bus to the Occoquan Workhouse. When we got there, we had an immediate discussion with the other women and told them our decision. There was already a group of either eight or twelve of our women there. They were very enthusiastic about the idea and accepted it, without question. The next day we appeared in the workroom and we just sat there with our hands in our laps.

All the women in that sewing room took an example from us. I think there were probably about a dozen other women in that room. When they saw that we weren't working, they took heart. They could be real courageous. They wouldn't work either. There was nothing that could be done about the whole room. I think that's what bothered the superintendent. He wouldn't have cared so much if the others had continued to work.

We'd go to the workroom and we'd just sit there all day long. We talked, you know. All we could do was talk. Since we were all sitting at one table, we did a great deal of talking as to how to comport ourselves. We lived in dormitories; we slept in one long dormitory with beds on both sides, about three feet apart from each other. It was just like the ones you see in motion pictures of prison wards or hospitals. There were about thirty in the dormitory—not just suffragists, but other prisoners, too. We took turns washing ourselves every morning. There were several sinks and we took turns. Then we went into the dining room.

I think twice a day we went out for our "constitutional." We had certain prescribed prison walks through the gardens there; it was a lovely fall time of the year, you know. The leaves were turning red and they were falling; the air was fresh.

The food was the greatest problem we had there. It was just unbelievable—the worms that were found in the oatmeal we ate, in the soup we ate. I don't remember anything else. The coffee was God knows what—it wasn't coffee. It might have been chicory. To me, that was the most terrible part of the whole prison experience, the food.

We all suffered. This was before the hunger strike, but some of the women were actually on a hunger strike already! They just couldn't eat. The only thing they could eat was bread, if it wasn't totally moldy and if it didn't show rat tracks.

The next group that came in was the one that went on a hunger strike, and they were brutally treated. They received very severe treatment. They were beaten and dragged across the patio from the superintendent's office to their cells. (These later women were segregated; they were put in cells.) Some women had broken ribs and were bleeding profusely and they weren't treated. Others had all kinds of lacerations.

After we were released from jail we went back to headquarters. I don't know how long I stayed there, perhaps another week or two. I was even tempted to go back again on the picket line, but I just couldn't stand the thought of going back to that workhouse again. After thirty days of that dreadful food and the fear of what might happen to the next contingent that was arrested, I just wasn't courageous enough to go back again. I felt horrified by the different things that could happen to you in prison. It wasn't as exciting as I had thought it would be; it was exciting in a frightening way, but not exciting in a joyous way. That was one reason why I decided not to go back again on the picket line and then be tried again and sentenced again.

After I came out of prison I had much more awareness of feminism and suffragette-ism than I did before then.

Sherna Gluck, *From Parlor to Prison* (New York: Vintage, 1976)

Sent into Exile

When America entered World War I, President Woodrow Wilson preached that the war was "a crusade to save the world for democracy." But the war had the strange effect of crippling democracy at home. As American troops joined the battle, a reign of terror was launched against those who opposed the war. Some dissented because they were pacifists or radicals, others because of their ethnic sympathies. Antiwar talk became dangerous. New espionage and sedition laws spurred informers on; their victims were whipped, tarred and feathered, and some even lynched. The attorney general, A. Mitchell Palmer, ordered federal agents to conduct a mass roundup of "Reds." In one night his men raided thirty-three cities and netted over 4,000 "suspected" radicals, most of them immigrants. Many were deported "back where they came from" or jailed for twenty-year sentences. Left-wing and ethnic newspapers were forced to close down.

One of the best-known victims of the Red Scare was Emma Goldman. Born in Russia in 1869, she came to America at sixteen, found work in a garment factory for $2.50 a week, and when she experienced the gap between the promise of equality and the harsh poverty and injustice working people endured, joined the anarchist movement. One of the country's most dynamic women speakers, she crisscrossed the land lecturing on anarchism, modern writers, and the revolt of women. She waged countless fights for free speech and often went to jail for her beliefs.

In June 1917 she was arrested for leading the opposition to conscription and sentenced to two years in prison. After her release in the fall of 1919, immigration officials ordered her deported to Russia. Just before Christmas, with 248 other victims of the Red Scare, she sailed past the Statue of Liberty aboard a government transport.

At a federal hearing on her deportation order, held in New York on October 27, 1919, Emma Goldman told what she believed in and protested what the government was doing to punish dissenters.

At the very outset of this hearing I wish to register my protest against these star-chamber proceedings, whose very spirit is nothing less than a revival of the ancient days of the Spanish Inquisition or the more recently defunct Third Degree system of Czarist Russia.

This star-chamber hearing is, furthermore, a denial of the insistent claim on the part of the government that in this country we have free speech and a free press, and that every offender against the law—even the lowliest of men— is entitled to his day in open court, and to be heard and judged by a jury of his peers.

If the present proceedings are for the purpose of proving some alleged offense committed by me, some evil or anti-social act, then I protest against the secrecy and third-degree methods of this so-called "trial." But if I am not charged with any specific offense or act, if—as I have reason to believe—this is purely an inquiry into my social and political opinions, then I protest still more vigorously against these proceedings, as utterly tyrannical and diametrically opposed to the fundamental guarantees of a true democracy.

Every human being is entitled to hold any opinion that appeals to her or him without making herself or himself liable to persecution. Ever since I have been in this country—and I have lived here practically all my life—it has been dinned into my ears that under the institutions of this alleged democracy one is entirely free to think and feel as he pleases. What becomes of this sacred guarantee of freedom of thought and conscience when persons are being persecuted and driven out for the very motives and purposes for which the pioneers who built up this country laid down their lives?

And what is the object of this star-chamber proceeding, that is admittedly based on the so-called anti-anarchist law [of 1903]? Is not the only purpose of this law, and of the deportations en masse, to suppress every symptom of popular discontent now manifesting itself through this country, as well as in all the European lands? It requires no great prophetic gift to foresee that this new governmental policy of deportation is but the first step toward the introduction into this country of the old Russian system of exile for the high treason of entertaining new ideas of social life and industrial reconstruction. Today so-called aliens are deported; tomorrow native Americans will be banished. Already some patrioteers are suggesting that native American sons, to whom democracy is not a sham but a sacred ideal, should be exiled. To be sure, America does not yet possess

122

EMMA GOLDMAN'S

FIVE SUNDAY NIGHT LECTURES

AT 43 EAST 22nd STREET

NEW YORK

AUTHOR:
ANARCHISM AND OTHER ESSAYS
PUBLISHER OF **MOTHER EARTH** MAGAZINE

Nov. 19. Communism, the most practical Basis for Society.
Nov. 26. Mary Wollstoncraft the pioneer of modern womanhood.
Dec. 3. Socialism caught in the political trap.
Dec. 10. Sex, the great element of creative work.
Dec. 17. Farewell lecture.

Meetings will begin at 8 P. M.   Questions and Discussion

Admission 25c.   *Tickets on sale at* **Mother Earth, 55 W. 28th St.**

   Sachs & Steinfeld. Union Printers. 12 Jefferson St.

A leaflet announcing a lecture series by Emma Goldman, who was at the time editing MOTHER EARTH, *the magazine she founded in 1906.*

a suitable place like Siberia to which her exiled sons might be sent, but since she has begun to acquire colonial possessions, in contradiction of the principles she stood for for over a century, it will not be difficult to find an American Siberia once the precedent of banishment is established. . . .

Under the mask of the same anti-anarchist law every criticism of a corrupt administration, every attack on governmental abuse, every manifestation of sympathy with the struggle of another country in the pangs of a new birth—in short, every free expression of untrammeled thought may be suppressed utterly, without even the semblance of an unprejudiced hearing or a fair trial. It is for these reasons, chiefly, that I strenuously protest against this despotic law and its star-chamber methods of procedure. I protest against the whole spirit underlying it—the spirit of an irresponsible hysteria, the result of the terrible war, and of the evil tendencies of bigotry and persecution and violence which are the epilogue of five years of bloodshed. . . .

Nowhere at Home: Letters from Exile of Emma Goldman and Alexander Berkman, Richard and Anna Maria Drinnon, eds. (New York: Schocken, 1975)

Chicago Style

By the 1920s the children of the east European Jewish immigrants were losing their distinctive traits as they rapidly absorbed the manners, the style, the language, and the morals of American culture. The Yiddish press lost masses of readers and scarcely one out of four Jews declared Yiddish as their mother tongue. In the 1920s they still preferred big-city life—most stayed in the Northeast—but they sought "better" neighborhoods than the ghettos.

Anti-Semitism restricted not only choice of residence, but also opportunities for jobs, especially white-collar. The ambitious looked to education and more education as the key to success. Here, too, quotas severely limited Jews. Nevertheless, between 1890 and 1925 Jewish enrollment in colleges grew at a rate five times greater than that of the general population. Jewish students in those years sought careers first in business and finance and then in medicine, engineering, law, and dentistry.

Of course not all young Jews desired or were able to attend college. The love of sports and hero worship of star athletes became as much a mania for Jews as it was for others. The children of the ghetto also dreamed of stardom as boxers, pitchers, and halfbacks. While some slaved over the piano or violin, aspiring to Carnegie Hall, others turned to jazz, a new and developing American music the whole world would cherish.

Richard Voynow was one of the jazz makers. A pianist in the early 1920s, he became manager of the famed Wolverines, one of the earliest white groups to play Dixieland. The Wolverines then included the jazz immortal Bix Beiderbecke. Voynow recalls those days in an interview given about a decade later.

Jazz was played long before this craze about it came into being. Nobody made too big a fuss about it. There is nothing that is being done today that wasn't done by the boys in my band or by the New Orleans Rhythm Kings. That outfit was the real influence on Chicago style. In fact, the bands today aren't even playing as good as my band was playing back in 1923, because we had Beiderbecke in our band and nobody has been able to touch him since. The other day I was down at Nick's in the Village and Bobby Hackett— he plays just like Bix, almost a perfect imitator—came up to me and said, "Listen to me, will you, Dick, and tell me if I do anything that Bix didn't do." I listened to him for some time and he did almost everything Bix did, but he wasn't as good, nor did he have Bix's originality.

Bix was really a genius. He was the kind of guy who would never send his clothes to a laundry. Never thought

125

of it. He would throw his stuff into a closet and leave it there and rummage through for a clothes change, and finally some guy in the band would get disgusted and send his clothes to the laundry. But he was a true artist. Sometimes we would go down to the Art Institute and although he knew nothing about painting from books, he would always stop in front of the best paintings and point them out and admire them. Bix had a fine feel for color tone on his horn, too. He was doing things musically, along with some of the other boys in the band, without even being conscious of it. The men in the Wolverines were all fine musicians who didn't play notes but created them.

I was the worst musician in the band but was the business head. All the boys knew that I was the worst musician, but they also felt they needed me to keep them together and to discipline them. We would have to make a train at nine-thirty, say, and I'd be waiting at the station for them, and they'd get off on a drinking spree or a love-fest or something, and come running half dressed to the station just when the train was pulling out. Things like that were enough to drive a guy crazy. But I had a better musical training than all of them. I'd do the skeleton arrangements during rehearsals. But you never had to tell them what to do, even though most of the fellows couldn't read a note. They'd pick up a tune from the melodies I'd knock out on the piano and then in their solos they'd create around that melody so that the music came out like a work of art. In the ensembles they never got lost but stayed in and played in perfect harmony.

Although Bix *felt* more when he played, there was a man called Teschemacher who played clarinet, who was also a genius, but who had a calculated manner of playing. He was an intellectual compared to the others—he knew the value of each note he hit, and knew why he played them. He had a marvelous musical background, which most of

126

the others didn't have, and it didn't hamper him any.

Because of Bix we couldn't stand anything but a cornet in our band. When Bix left the band, we were almost driven to distraction trying to get someone who could really fit in. We tried out a few but they didn't do. We even brought up Sharkey Bonano from New Orleans. He walked in with a trumpet and all the fellows shook their heads. Sharkey played fine trumpet, but we had got so used to the cornet because of Bix we just couldn't see a trumpet. Finally one of the boys in the band said that he had heard a kid from Chicago play who sounded pretty good. We sent for the kid and he turned out to be Jimmy McPartland. We were very happy to get him because he filled Bix's place pretty well and he was so influenced by Bix he worked in fine right off the bat. But he could never excel Bix.

Ann Banks, *First Person America* (New York: Knopf, 1980)

Just Enough Religion

In the 1920s the Ku Klux Klan rose again to threaten American democracy. First organized in the South after the Civil War, the aim of the secret society was to restore the old slaveholders to power. With poor whites as its troops, the Klan overthrew the new democratic state governments by force and violence. After World War I, when economic and social troubles again disturbed the nation, the Klan was reborn. In the early twenties, government scandals arose over the exploitation of public lands by oil interests. Rumrunners and bootleggers like Al Capone prospered as the manufacture, transportation, and sale of alcoholic liquors were prohibited. Public cynicism lifted such gangsters to great power in the world's of politics and business. Millions played the stock *market in a speculative fever. But four out of five familes made less than $3000 a year and 6 million families had incomes under $1000 a year.*

Whole regions of the country suffered hard times, while farmers everywhere did poorly. Nativists blamed the troubles on the millions of immigrants entering the country, and in 1924 Congress voted to end mass immigration. The Klan at this time posed as a force for stability. It claimed to stand for "100 percent Americanism," attacking Blacks, Jews, Catholics, the unions, and anyone who believed in equality. It recruited millions of followers from a country confused by the uncertainty of the times. Because of color, creed, or beliefs, Klan victims suffered economic boycott, social ostracism, and every form of harrassment and intimidation that a bigoted group can use.

The Klan grew very powerful, especially in the South, Midwest, and West. Parades of robed and hooded Ku Kluxers carrying burning crosses terrorized communities, staging hundreds of floggings and tar-and-feather parties. It took courage to speak and act against the KKK. One such brave man was Rabbi Morris Feuerlicht, who spent nearly fifty years in the pulpit of the Indianapolis Hebrew Congregation. Born in 1879 in Hungary, he graduated from Hebrew Union College in Cincinnati in 1901. He became the first Jewish member of the Indiana Board of Charities and Correction in 1920. At this time, the Klan was the dominant political power in his state and many others. For a decade the organization was able to elect senators and congressmen, governors, state legislators, mayors, city councilmen, and sheriffs. In this memoir the rabbi recalls clashes with the Klan.

Chief targets of the Klan agitation in Indiana were Roman Catholics, on religious grounds primarily, and Jews, for business reasons usually inspired by envious non-Jewish local competitors. But the curious thing about it all was that the agitation was noisiest in communities where Catholics and Jews were fewest in number, if not altogether absent. My own disturbed state of mind throughout this period can readily be imagined. It was shared, of course, not only by my fellow Jews and the other victims of the Klan propaganda, but also by all the decent and high-minded citizens of the state. In the face of blazing fiery crosses and brazen terrorist tactics, however, they appeared to be able only to stand by and await developments.

Klan terrorism made any kind of active resistance short of rioting and shooting warfare seem futile. Here and there a few voices did speak out. More eagerly perhaps than under normal conditions, I accepted invitations to address service, business, church, and women's organizations throughout the state, groups which wanted to hear some kind of pronouncements from the minority or unpopular side of the subject. And I was supposed to be especially and personally complimented by such invitations, because in only the rarest instances, if any, had similar invitations been tendered to a representative of the other three Klan opposition groups. Of course, I took advantage of such opportunities to satirize the Klan's percentage kind of Americanism, and to appeal to the better judgment and higher patriotism of my hearers. Invariably, the first to come up at the conclusion of the address for a word of appreciation would be some self-announced Catholics, to be followed rather timidly by others.

To show that we in Indianapolis at least were not yet completely intimidated by all this Klan agitation, two mass meetings of protest were held in Cadle Tabernacle, a supposed Klan stronghold. These were addressed by two prominent Protestant ministers. . . . Both meetings were sponsored and arranged by a small but loosely organized committee of local Roman Catholics, Protestants, and Jews which ultimately grew into what is now known as the National Conference of Christians and Jews. . . .

This was one of the very few instances of my ministry in which I felt it was not only warranted as a citizen but also was my duty as a rabbi to take a dip into the frequently complicated practices of real party politics. A somewhat more dramatic instance, but one involving Jews more directly, occurred during this same Klan period at Muncie, the very head and center of the movement in Indiana. An upstart lawyer by the name of Clarence Dearth had announced himself Republican candidate for county judge on a Klan platform. Here, too, both Republican and Klan sentiment appeared to be in the majority. To offset and, if possible, defeat this candidate, the Democratic organization prevailed upon Adolph Silverburg, a leading lawyer and the outstanding Jew of Muncie, to accept their nomination as Dearth's opponent. Reluctantly he accepted, primarily, as he expressed it, as a matter of party loyalty and plain decency. The organization well knew his sincerity in this, because he had neither the taste nor the need for dabbling in local politics, but he in turn was convinced of his party's honesty in trying to maintain the good name of the city against the threat of Klanism. In the preelection campaign, Dearth ambulated about the county, haranguing his audiences and denouncing his opponent in the most vulgar and demagogical terms. "Do you want a miserable Jew to sit in judgment upon you?" he insistently and shamelessly challenged. The election returns favored Dearth, and Silverburg, as can well be understood, felt bitterly humiliated.

A few weeks later, the handful of Jewish families in Muncie, about fifty in a total population of some thirty thousand, dedicated their small new synagogue. All the city's notables were invited to attend the ceremonies. Muncie had been my monthly pulpit in student days. Accordingly, for this reason, as well as my being rabbi of the temple in the state capital, I was invited to deliver the dedicatory address. Silverburg was chairman of the building committee and in that capacity was to present the keys of the building to the president. In doing so he recited in a loud but quavering voice just a single line for his speech: *"Shema yisroel adonoy elobenuadonoy echod*—Hear, O Israel, the Lord our God, the Lord is One! For that idea," he continued, "I have been crucified." He then handed the keys to the president and abruptly took his seat.

The effect upon the assembly was literally stunning. It seemed as if a wave of mingled shock and guilt was visibly sweeping through and across his audience. My address immediately followed, so it devolved upon me somehow to allay as best I could the very perceptible uneasiness of the moment. I managed to sputter something about our common understanding of Silverburg's feelings in the light of what had so recently occurred in the community. Then I proceeded with my prepared address, reminding my audience, however, that once upon a time, about two centuries ago, Dean Swift had written: "Some people have just enough religion to hate their fellowmen, but not enough religion to love them"—whereupon the mayor of the city, who was sitting directly beneath my eye, impulsively punched his neighbor on the knee and quite audibly remarked: "See, that's just what I've been telling you fellows all along."

Muncie, however, even amid such unflattering incidents, was not yet completely Klan-ridden. It should be recorded that the well-known family of Ball Brothers, glass manufacturers, contributed the unsolicited sum of five thousand dollars to the building fund of the Muncie synagogue. The family contributed a like amount for a similar purpose in nearby Marion. Moreover, in the infamous Dearth episode a day of poetic justice for Silverburg was not far in the offing. Not long after Dearth took his seat on the bench, he was charged with malfeasance in office, was tried, found guilty, and finally removed by a special session of the state legislature called for the purpose. There still persists, however, a strange and malodorous aftermath of Klanism in Indiana, despite this public finding of the legislature. A transcript of the legislature's proceedings somehow disappeared shortly after the single day's trial session, and to this day (1953) has not been recovered. Thus, so far as the state's official records are concerned, the whole Dearth episode remains a historical blank.

Stanley F. Chyet, ed., *Lives and Voices,* Jewish Publication Society, 1972

Artists
in Their Line

Outside the garment industry, Jews worked in a rich variety of occupations. They were carpenters and cabinetmakers, metalworkers and printers, plumbers and mechanics, blacksmiths and watchmakers. They were furriers, jewelers, bookbinders, electricians, masons, roofers, locksmiths. Others did not work with their hands, but lived by trading—peddlers, shopkeepers, merchants, dealers. Ambitious parents—and few were not— urged their children to become professionals—librarians, teachers, pharmacists, dentists, doctors, lawyers.

The father of Alfred Kazin was a house painter. Raised in Brooklyn in the twenties and thirties, young Kazin observed the precarious life of the immigrant workers.

Every Saturday morning about eleven my father and his fellow house painters gathered in one circle, carpenters and plasterers and bricklayers in theirs. The men came to talk shop, and if they were out of work, to get the nod from the union delegate or a boss, who walked about in the crowd calling hands to a new job. . . .

132

I liked listening to the painters talk about their famous union boss, Jake the Bum, and to the unending disputes between left wing and right wing, which had been in friction with each other for so long, [which] so automatically bristled and flared as soon as a word was said, that the embattled daily life of the union came alive for me. I liked especially hearing the men roll out those long curses against the "boss painters"—*may a black year befall them, the miserable bastards*—which made up, a little, for the insecurity of their trade. I was happy my father was a painter; I liked painters. They were not bent and cadaverous and pale, like my uncles and cousins in the garment lofts on Seventh Avenue; the smell of paint and plaster was still on their overcoats Saturday mornings; they had a kind of mock bravado that suited men who were always getting up on scaffolds and falling off scaffolds and rising off the ground with a curse to live another day; and who liked to think of themselves as great drinkers and boasters and lechers, knew how to laze on a job, how to drive an unpopular contractor crazy; thought of themselves all as great artists in their line; and never knew from one month to the next if they would be working, or where.

I can still hear my mother's anxious question each time my father returned from that labor pool in front of the Municipal Bank—*Geyst arbeten?* Will there be work this week? From the early 'thirties on, my father could never be sure in advance of a week's work. Even the "long" jobs never seemed to last very long, and if he was on an "outside" job, a rainy day was a day lost. It puzzled me greatly when I came to read in books that Jews are a shrewd people particularly given to commerce and banking, for all the Jews I knew had managed to be an exception to that rule. I grew up with the belief that the natural condition of a Jew was to be a propertyless worker like my painter father and my dressmaker mother and my dressmaker uncles and cousins in Brownsville—workers, kin to all the workers of the world, dependent entirely on the work of their hands. All happiness in our house was measured by the length of a job. The greatest imaginable bliss was a "busy season." It was unfortunate, but did not matter too much, if the boss was a bastard, a skinflint, a cheat, a no-good, so sharp with his men that one might—God forgive us—doubt that he was a Jew. All that was to be expected of him, was of his very essence as a boss—for a boss, as my mother once off-handedly defined the type in a sentence that lighted up for me our instinctive belief in the class struggle—a boss was a man who did nothing himself, sat by idly, enjoying himself, and got rich on the bitter toil of others. It was far more important to us that the boss be successful, full of work to give out. Let him be mean, let him be unspeakable, let him be hateful—he kept us alive. I remember it was said of a young painter cousin of mine, who had somehow managed to work six months steady, that he lived on his boss, meaning that there was something suspect about him; it was as if he had morally deserted the working class by getting too close to the boss—for how else could he have managed that triumph?

Alfred Kazin, *A Walker in the City* (New York: Harcourt Brace Jovanovich, 1951)

Rock Bottom

The thirties was the time when I was growing up. As the decade of the Great Depression opened, I had entered my second year of high school. My hometown—Worcester, Massachusetts, an industrial city of 200,000 people—would suffer hard times like the rest of America.

134

By the end of 1932 the depression had devastated the nation for three long years. Fourteen million were unemployed. The Jews were part of that appalling statistic. Thousands of Jewish businesses went bankrupt. Doctors and dentists lost patients, storekeepers lost customers, landlords lost rents, lawyers lost clients, workers in a crippled garment industry lost jobs. Many of the east European immigrant minority who had struck it rich in the twenties were ruined.

My father and mother, immigrants from Austro-Hungary, had little education and no trade or profession. For a living my father cleaned the windows of factories, stores, offices, and homes. In a memoir of those years, I recorded what happened to us and our neighbors.

As factories cut down production and stores were boarded up, there were fewer and fewer windows to clean. My father, whose day began at two in the morning and often did not end until late afternoon, was home more and more for lack of work. Extra jobs, even the oddest ones, were hard to find. The telephone company fired twenty married women because their husbands had jobs. The best my older brother, my mother, and I could do was to get part-time work that lasted briefly and paid poorly. Still, we managed to eat. Food was cheaper then, and the Depression drove prices even lower. At the corner grocery, eggs were 19 cents a dozen; lettuce, a nickel a head; whole-wheat bread, a nickel a loaf; bananas, 8 cents a dozen; mackerel, two pounds for a quarter; beef, 11 cents a pound; and tomato soup, three cans for 19 cents.

By the winter of 1931, there were men in our neighborhood who had been out of work for months. When Lake Quinsigamond froze, my friend's father was lucky enough to get temporary work harvesting the ice in a crew of jobless men hired by the city employment bureau.

And relief, what was that? There were no plans for public welfare. There was no such thing as unemployment insurance. . . .

The sense of injured pride that afflicted many unemployed workers in the 1930's is expressed on this jobless Detroiter's face as well as on the homemade sign he carries.
THE DETROIT News

A sign of the Great Depression on the streets of Detroit. THE DETROIT NEWS

By my last year in high school, 1932, one-fourth of the nation—men, women, and children—belonged to families with no regular income. And almost nothing was being done to provide them with relief. Wealthy businessmen were against any national measure that would raise their federal income tax.

The cities, counties, and states were not prepared to meet the crisis. Even when they meant well, few had enough funds to offer relief. Where they did, many proud people refused to take it. They believed it was their own fault if they lost a job. They were ashamed to accept help. . . .

In the Worcester *Telegram* I read about a man who had

gone into a downtown restaurant, ordered oysters, salad, a steak, pie, ice cream, and coffee. After finishing his meal, he called the manager and said, "Now you can put me in jail. This was my first meal in three days. I haven't got a dime."

A few days later, our newspaper reported that a twenty-two-year-old man had shot his fiancée, killing her when she returned his engagement ring. Her parents had forced her to break off with him because he had failed to find work for more than a year, and had no prospects. . . .

Eight inches of snow fell toward the end of that year of 1931. A blessing for the jobless. The city hired those with dependent families to clear the streets. . . .

Perhaps as a generous Christmas gesture, City Hall announced that twenty-six more men would be given apple-selling posts. There were so many men out on the streets selling apples for a nickel apiece that Worcester had to regulate the trade.

It was our senior year in high school. Some of the kids joked about whether the school would last long enough to let us graduate. After all, Chicago, an infinitely bigger city, had just shut down its schools because of lack of funds. Their teachers had not been paid for months.

In February, a young, university-trained actress, who had gone to Broadway full of hope and ambition, came back to Worcester. She had failed to find even a walk-on role in a starving theater. She sat silently at home for a few weeks, then took a trolley car out to Lake Quinsigamond, chopped a hole in the ice, and drowned herself.

The last story of that winter I care to remember is that of Albert Fortin and Pasquale Furtaldo. Albert, twenty-three, had not eaten for several days. He saw Pasquale, fifteen, leave a grocery store carrying a loaf of bread and a bottle of milk. He followed the boy home and as Pasquale was about to enter his house, seized an ax and struck him on the head. Frightened by his own violence, he dragged the boy to the rear of the house, and then fled, without the bread and milk. A few hours later he surrendered to the police.

Milton Meltzer, *Violins and Shovels* (New York: Delacorte, 1976)

A Job at Macy's

In the thirties, the American Jewish community was made up of a minority of German Jews and a much larger majority of east Europeans. Those of German origin were mostly middle or upper class. Wealthy Jews were only a thin layer atop the Jewish millions. Almost all had started in poverty. The few who made it could forget where they had come from. The Jewish business world was ghettoized then; Jews produced for Jews and sold for and to Jews. The patients of Jewish doctors were usually Jews and so were the clients of Jewish lawyers. The trades and businesses that served Jews were also generally made up of Jews.

Macy's, the largest department store in New York and (it boasted) the world, was Jewish-owned, but it hired people of all faiths. With jobs so scarce, even college graduates felt they were lucky to find work there. Irving Fajans, an organizer for a union of department store workers, sold merchandise behind the counters of many New York stores, including Macy's. In an interview with the Federal Writers Project, he described the working conditions at Macy's and then recalled the famous sit-down strike the employees of the Grand chain stores staged in 1937.

When you first get a job at Macy's, they start you in the stock room. I was two years out of high school when I got on there and I worked for Macy's five years. Not all the time in stock—I did some selling on the floor too, and I worked in the tube room, where they make change. You're lucky if you get out of stock. Some guys have been there twenty, twenty-five years. They learn one routine job in one department, and then even if they move on to other houses, they'll be placed on the same job because of experience. A few of them get into other departments if the boss figures they got something on the ball—which isn't often.

All Macy's employees have to take intelligence tests before they're hired; the same thing goes for most of the larger houses. Funny thing about those tests, they don't hire you if your average is too high—not to start anyway. If your quotient runs between ninety and one-hundred-ten, you'll get by easier. They figure if a worker's too smart, he's liable to get a notion he doesn't like the way things are done and maybe start the others to getting dissatisfied, too. On the other hand, if he's too dumb, he can't handle the job. So don't be too smart or too dumb.

In Macy's the stock takes up eight floors and they have a warehouse a whole block square. The merchandise comes in on trucks, is unloaded on the receiving platform, and then sent to the stock rooms. Then the checkers look it over, mark down the quantity, and report any damages. After that, it's priced—price tags, pin tickets, gum labels, or string labels put on—then it's sent to the reserve. The reserve room is just long aisles of shelves, where the pickers and distributors classify the stock. When the merchandise is ordered from the selling floor, it's either sent down the chutes or taken down on small floor trucks, or "wheelers." They use mostly women for markers and examiners, that is to examine the stock for flaws and for marking the quantity. The pickers and distributors and truckers are all men. It's one hell of a job sometimes to keep up with the orders from the floor. You've got to run along the shelves, grab the order, and load the trucks or shove it down the chute.

Irving Fajans, an organizer of department store workers in New York. Soon after the sit-down strike in 1937, he joined the International Brigades to fight against fascism in Spain. COURTESY OF MIMI ROCKMORE

Lots of times it'll be a "Customer Waiting" order, and that means hurry it up. They ought to put the guys on roller skates; maybe then they'd get the right kind of speed out of them.

There's a supervisor to each floor, who's generally snooping around hoping to catch you loafing on the job. Mostly the workers call them "supers"; when I was there, we called them "snoopers." One super we had was a tough guy. He had a voice like a dog's bite and he was proud of the way he could lash speed out of the boys picking stock. One Christmas, we all chipped in and bought him a horse whip, one of those old-fashioned ones. He must have caught on to the idea O.K. because he came back after the holidays with a pretty sour face, and gave us tougher treatment than before.

Working conditions are much better in Macy's now than when I used to work there. The place has been fairly well unionized. When I first started there, they were just beginning to try to organize, and everything pertaining to the union had to be on the q.t. If you were caught distributing leaflets or other union literature around the job you were instantly fired. We thought up ways of passing leaflets without the boss being able to pin anybody down. Sometimes we'd insert the leaflets into the sales ledgers after closing time. In the morning every clerk would find a pink sheet saying: "Good morning, how's everything . . . and how about coming to union meeting tonight?" or something like that. We swiped the key to the toilet-paper dispenser in the washroom, took out the paper, and substituted printed slips of just the right size! We got a lot of new members that way—it appealed to their sense of humor. We also used to toss a bunch of leaflets down the store chutes with the merchandise when the super had his back turned. They'd all scatter on the receiving end, and the clerks would pick them up when they handled the stock. The floorwalker might see those pink sheets all over the place and get sore as hell—but what could he do? No way of telling who did it.

[Fajans talks about the Grand strike.]

The management had refused to negotiate with our committee, and the workers voted for a sit-in to demand shorter hours and better working conditions. The whistles were blown in every Grand store in New York at eleven-thirty A.M. on March 14th. The workers finished their sales and folded their arms, refusing to wait on any more customers. Practically a hundred percent of the workers joined us, and most of the stores immediately closed their doors. We were prepared to stay a month if necessary.

We had cots brought in and blankets, electric burners for coffee, and plenty of eats. There was food and other things we might have used in the store, but none of our people touched any sort of merchandise during the strike. It was pretty cold, being early spring, so we had to huddle together at night. There were some canary cages in the store, and we kept the birds fed; they'd wake us up every morning. We had games like checkers and cards, and we had a radio and danced to the music.

Two engagements were announced during the time we sat in. We even held a marriage ceremony there for a couple who decided to get married during the strike: the girls dressed up the bride; we sent for a priest and he married them. The strike held out over Easter week and since some of our people were Italians and Irish Catholics, we held Easter services for them in the store.

Nobody left the store for eleven days except the committee to contact the management. The girls held out just as well as the fellows, and everyone tried to be gay and have as good a time as possible. Luckily, no one in our store got sick during the strike. The management finally heard our committee and met our demands—largely as a result of the publicity our sit-down had gotten all over the country.

During the Ohrbach's strike a couple of years ago, two salesgirls pulled a neat stunt. Mr. Ohrbach, who is supposed to be a big philanthropist, spoke at a dinner held for him at the Hotel Astor. While he was spouting about some of these public charity funds, two girls who had crashed the dinner in borrowed evening gowns climbed up on the balcony and chained themselves to the railing. Nobody noticed them, and suddenly they began shouting in the middle of Ohrbach's speech: "Charity begins at home! Give your employees shorter hours and better pay!" Of course, there was a big hubbub, and the girls were arrested. But the papers carried a big story, and the boss had to grant our demands to appease public opinion.

Banks, *First Person America*

A Reason for Dying

In July of 1936, General Francisco Franco led an armed revolt against the democratic republic of Spain, initiating the Spanish civil war. The war went on for more than three years and ended in the overthrow of the legal government. Adolf Hitler and Benito Mussolini, the fascist dictators of Germany and Italy, sent troops and arms to help Franco, while most of the world stood by, watching the Spanish democracy die.

Although their governments refused aid to the Spanish Loyalists struggling for survival, tens of thousands of volunteers from dozens of countries rallied to help the Spanish people, joining the International Brigades in the fight for freedom. Among them were 3,300 Americans, of many ethnic groups including Jews. About 1,800 of the American volunteers lost their lives. Alvah Bessie, a Jewish American writer, joined the American Lincoln Brigade in Spain. What he did, and why, he tells in these passages from Men in Battle, *his book about the war.*

143

We were crouched in the shallow *refugios* alongside the cliff; I was lying on my back and Dick was catching a little sleep at my feet, with Archie behind him with Sans. It had just passed noon when they opened up, and from the start they had our range. We could count about seven batteries at work, all of them concentrated on our sector, that was no more than five hundred yards wide. They began coming over, and we stayed down; they came, you heard them from the start to the end, the three low harmless thumps of the faraway guns, then a brief silence, then a low hissing growing crescendo into a riffling whistle (a scream if they were coming close) and then a deafening crash that reverberated between the two slopes that enclosed the *baranco* behind the hill. We stuck our heads up to see where they had landed, saw the brown and white smoke drifting away, the rocks falling as though in slow motion, possibly a couple men running. Then they were coming again and we ducked again.

"That was close," Curtis said. "They've got us spotted."

He was in the next hole with the telephonist, Felix. I turned onto my back, saw Aaron's automatic pistol tucked between the two rocks where I had put it, still streaked with his dried blood. (Doc Simon had sent word that he would be all right.) I heard them coming again, and closed my eyes, put my arms over my face and waited. You felt nothing at such moments except a tightening of the belly, and you drew up your legs instinctively and then it was all over. There were occasional duds; occasionally a shell whistling close overhead would suddenly lose its twirling motion and, turning end over end, go scuffling through the air making a noise like a small boy blowing air between his lips. You wanted to laugh when you heard those.

"Oh, Christ," said Curtis, "this is awful!"

"Shut up!"

"Why, what's the matter?"

"Nobody likes it any more than you do."

From where I was lying, if I lifted my head, I could see the built-up parapets of the other men in the *plana mayor,* the stretcher-bearers, the barber, the quartermaster Lara. When the shells were coming they were nowhere to be seen; after they had landed and the shrapnel had stopped screeching and smacking at the stone, they all sat up, sticking their heads over the parapet as though they were puppets in a Punch and Judy show. It was funny. Dick was crouched in front of me, with Archie behind him and Sans lying on his face the other way. "What about it?" Archie yelled, and Dick shouted, "What about what?" "We ought to be up in the line," the commissar said; then they both ducked and the thing went off and deafened us and the stones fell in on us from where the shrapnel and concussion had chipped away the cliff.

There was a terrific tearing smash and everything was black and a voice was screaming, screaming. I went out for a moment and came to, and put my hand on top of my head and looked at my hand, but there was no blood on it. It was difficult to see, the air was clogged with rock dust and smoke and the ringing was continuous and the voice kept screaming on a high note. Far away, I heard Dick say, "Who got it? You, Bess?" and I said, "I don't think so," and sat up. The screaming came from behind me, so I got up and looked, and there was Curtis, lying on his belly, his buttocks torn away, holding them with his hands, his face turned to me, dead white and powdered with rock dust, and his mouth open, his eyes looking at me, his mouth open screaming. I could not take my eyes away from his.

"Come on!" Archie shouted, and he and Dick ducked out and up the hill.

Felix lay behind Curtis, his legs bloody and his face still, and I climbed over the few stones that remained standing between us, and Felix said, "Take him first, he's worse." Curtis kept screaming although his mouth did not move, looking at me with his eyes wide and staring, and I was saying, "Take it easy take it easy take it easy," and suddenly it was *good* to be moving, good to be doing something instead of just lying there waiting for something to happen. I yelled for the *practicante,* but he was in the lines; I yelled for a bandage and was handed a small one-inch roll that was worthless. I called the stretcher-bearers, who came and we lifted Curtis out under the arms and knees (he was not screaming now), and they went away with him through the fire that was falling before us, behind us (Rafael was looking up over a near-by parapet, his mouth open), the noise terrific and the shrapnel whining and slapping around.

Felix's legs were badly torn and his foot was broken to bits, the bones stuck through the torn leather of his shoes. I gave him a cigarette (like in the movies) and tried with my wet red hands to light it for him, succeeding after a time. Rafael threw over a canteen of wine, and he took a slug or two. There was a pool of rapidly congealing blood, like half-stiffened Jello on the floor of the *refugio,* and I threw a blanket over it, spread the other over Felix and climbed back into my own hole. . . .

Planes came over, but they withheld their bombs, possibly because our lines were so close to theirs; you did not care. Time stood still—but absolutely. What do you think? What do you feel? Everything and nothing . . . saying over and over, "Dan and Dave stick with me now, and all the days to come, stick with me now." And it was astonishing, how you could not hold their image in your mind. . . .

The pauses were worse than the shelling, before and after, waiting for them to cool their guns. When they are dropping the mind is impersonal even if the body is not, but waiting for them to begin again. . . . A fly is attracted to your bloody hands and clothes; you shake it off. A louse is crawling in your groin and you think, At least you're safe, you louse, and laugh. Dry lips, rising gorge, sweat and shaking limbs. You look at your hands, filthy and covered with the blood of two men who have finally been taken where? You lie and insanely cover your face with your leather jacket when you hear them coming, as though it offered any protection. You throw it angrily from you, knowing yourself a fool, but grasp it again instinctively when the whistling is growing louder and your mind tells you *this* one will be close. Hour after hour, waiting for them to find you and finish you, waiting like a rat in a trap, chained to the command post by the commander's simple words, "I'll need you here." And chained by more—for you cannot run away from this struggle; it is everywhere; you could not look yourself in the face again. . . .

It all seems very far away and meaningless although you know the meaning or you would not be there; there is no immediate reality in this. You can think of Times Square with all its cars and all its people, and the focus narrows down and you can see their faces, ordinary commonplace faces like the faces you have known all your life, like the faces of the Spanish men and women and children you have seen in the cities and the small towns and the country, who are waiting back of the lines now, maybe reading a newspaper: Our forces in the Sector of X . . . repulsed, with heavy casualties, a violent enemy attack and withdrew to predetermined positions on Hill Z. . . . And what does that mean, tell me, and do you know? Faces. Do they care about us over there? And do they even think of us with love? The women and the children and the men: do they know we are so far away from them and dying for them? Do they know this is *their* struggle too? There is no connection between the fact of war and people; not when you are in it. It seems to be something taking place upon another, insulated plane of existence that does not, while you live it, touch the people whom it really touches. You think of love.

Yes, you can think of love. The love you have never had and could not give; the love that does not need words to create itself, but exists as a bond between the man and the woman who can look at each other and say inside their minds, I love and I am loved. The body is precious to you; the body wants to live. It wants to live to touch again . . . those tender parts of a woman's body that are so much of woman (her symbol and her essence), those parts you only need to touch so lightly with your hand to know again that you are a man and she is a woman and that there *is* a meaning to the world and to the life we try to live, but which they are trying to steal from us. For it is love alone that can, for even a moment of our time, give you the illusion that you are not alone, penetrate your loneliness and separate it from you for that moment. And you are afraid that you will die without that love; you are not just afraid to *die*. And this is the meaning of it all (the people's war); these men behind these fragile rocks, these men whose tender flesh is torn to pieces by the hot and ragged steel; they could not accept their death with such good grace if they did not love so deeply and so well—were not determined that love must come alive into the world. What other reason could there be for dying? What other reason for this blood upon your hands?

Alvah Bessie, *Men in Battle* (New York: Scribner's, 1939)

He Didn't Want to Know About Joseph

The worldwide economic crisis of the thirties made the terrible postwar conditions in Germany even worse. The Nazi party promised salvation on a program that blamed the Jews for most of the nation's troubles. By 1933 Adolf Hitler was able to take power and establish a dictatorship. The day he came into office, Carl Cohen, a mathematician and high school teacher, went underground to sabotage the Nazi rule. As a Jew and anti-Nazi he lost his job and lived on the earnings from private lessons. Although picked up by the police many times, he was not sent to a concentration camp until November 9, 1938—Kristallnacht—the nationwide pogrom in Germany triggered by the assassination of a German official in Paris. The Nazis burned most of the synagogues, ransacked and destroyed 7500 shops, looted and wrecked hundreds of homes. At least 1000 Jews were murdered, and 26,000—Carl Cohen among them—were forced into concentration camps.

Many of the victims of Nazism tried frantically to escape Hitler's reign of terror. But most countries, including the United States, did little to help rescue Europe's beleagured Jews. Between 1933 and the day America entered World War II, only 100,000 Jews were allowed into the States. Yet there were over 400,000 unfilled places within U.S. immigration quotas for countries under Nazi domination. America had forgotten its tradition of sanctuary for the oppressed.

In 1939, the Gestapo expelled Carl Cohen and his wife from Germany. (His parents died in a concentration camp.) The Cohens sailed for America, but at the port of entry were refused permission to come in. He tells what happened then.

Because my wife was paralyzed it was against the law to admit her. Paralyzed people, blind people, anarchists, prostitutes, inmates of lunatic asylums, and people who say "yes" to the question, "Would you kill the president of the United States?" I never heard of anybody answering "yes." Because of this they would not allow my wife to come in, and not me either, because they thought I would abandon my wife. Some such thing had happened before. People got married on paper, without consummating marriage, just to save somebody's life, and I'm not above it. I would have done it, too, but it so happens that I was in love with my wife.

I was there for five weeks. Then I got tired and sick of it and announced a hunger strike and sent a letter to Mrs. Roosevelt, the wife of the president. I lied—that I had a personal relationship to her, an introduction—that I was going to write to her on the basis of this introduction, asking her whether it was a crime in this country to be married to a paralyzed person. Mr. Roosevelt was also paralyzed, but I didn't say that. I said all this with tongue in cheek. That evening they got a telegram from Washington, D.C., that they should parole me. I said, "How about my wife?"

"Nothing about her. We'll still keep her."

So I didn't know what to do.

[Later she was allowed in.]

I got a job, which was floor-sweeping and toilet-bowl-cleaning in South Boston. As the floor-sweeper there I went through the whole establishment and asked everyone to tell me their stories, so I learned American society from the bottom, first the foreign prisoners, then with the very fine workers in the factory, later on other people.

I got my first teaching job on my own—Hebrew-teaching in Roxbury, which was then rather Jewish. This job also paid very, very little—about half of what we needed, $1,950 the year. This was in '41. During the war I tried to inform Jewish groups about Germany. They didn't listen. One of the reasons was because I was a Hebrew teacher and Hebrew teachers are regarded as very low-class.

German Jews were desperate, and the American Jews did not react. They could have given affidavits. This *might* have helped. They should have lied, "This man is my cousin," as the man in New York did for me. After all, when his grandmother was the second cousin of my step-great-grandmother, he was *not* my cousin. With this affidavit I got in. Why didn't a hundred thousand American Jews do it? Look, in the Bible there is the sentence, "A new king came up over Egypt who didn't know Joseph." You know what Joseph did for Egypt? The Talmud says, "He didn't want to know about Joseph." And that is the story of the American Jews.

And when I talked in Christian circles, it was unpleasant, too. Almost always someone came to me immediately after my talk with a friendly smile and said, "Aren't you happy you're in America!" And that cut me off.

During the war, when I taught soldiers, sailors, and civilians at Harvard, that was very gratifying. In my opinion, I contributed something: number one to victory and number two I told the students that Germans are like all other people. Germany is the country which gave me culture. My mother's family lived in the same city from 1470 on. When my friends and comrades in the underground were suffering in concentration camps, I could not forsake them. I made many enemies this way.

I want to tell you that my late wife and I were not permitted to send food. They wanted to starve the Germans, which was just what the Nazis did. Nazis wanted to kill the Jews, and they wanted to kill the Germans, so I told them, "You are Nazis." I get still angry when I think of it. So we made up our minds and we had very little money, maybe a thousand dollars, and we spent it on food packages. This was in '46, '47, when they were starving the Germans. Eventually it spread, other people did it too, but again we made enemies.

Well, all right, I was used to suffer for being a Jew and I didn't mind to suffer for being a German. I want to be with the underdog and suffer with him, and I have led a very happy life this way. I have got my satisfaction. Not in material ways, but I got it. And looking back now on a long, long life, I must say it was blessed.

June Namias, *First Generation* (Boston: Beacon, 1978)

A Killing Center

Corporal Howard Katzander, a Jewish American soldier, was with General George Patton's Third Army when it fought its way into Germany near the end of World War II. On an April day in 1945, the troops reached one of Hitler's death camps near the town of Weimar. Once the cultural heart of Germany, Weimar was the birthplace of the democratic republic that succeeded the German empire after its defeat in the First World War. Now, close by it, like some hideous sore, was a concentration camp called Buchenwald. It had been one of the first camps Hitler set up early in his regime to eliminate by terror every form of opposition to Nazism. Later, when Hitler began his war to exterminate the Jews, this and many other such camps became killing centers.

By the time the war ended, Hitler had murdered 6 million Jews, not because of their faith, but because of what he called their "race." He did not believe this "inferior" people had any right to share the earth with their "superiors"—the Germans. Two out of every three Jews in Europe, one-third of the world's Jews, died in the Holocaust.

When the American soldiers liberated Buchenwald, they found 21,000 starving survivors, as gaunt as corpses. For the armed services newspaper Yank, *Corporal Katzander wrote this first impression of what he saw that day.*

At Buchenwald concentration camp I saw bake ovens. Instead of being used to bake bread they were used to destroy people.

They were most efficient. Each was equipped with a door and a sliding board down which victims could be slipped to eventual destruction.

There were various stories about how the victims were knocked out before they were "baked," and I saw one club which had been used for that purpose. There was also a table where gold fillings were removed from the teeth of skulls.

A survivor of Hitler's Holocaust, photographed in the spring of 1945, when Allied troops liberated the death camps.

There were long steel stretchers on which the prisoners, often still alive, were rolled into the stinking heat of the ovens. I don't know how far German efficiency went, but

I'm sure the heat from so much good coke and so many tons of sizzling flesh could not have been wasted. Perhaps it was circulated through asbestos pipes to warm the quarters of the SS guards.

The Germans had an inspirational four-line stanza painted on a signboard in the cellar. The stanza explains that man does not want his body to be eaten by worms and insects; he prefers the purifying oblivion of flame.

Before purification the prisoners lived in barracks-like structures about 200 feet long. On either side of the buildings are four layers of shelves about five feet deep and three feet apart. Two-by-fours, spaced five feet apart, cut these building-long shelves into compartments. The final compartment is about five feet wide, five feet deep, two or three feet high.

In each of these compartments, the Germans put six men—or seven, when, as was normal, the camp was crowded.

And, remarkably enough, there is room for six or seven men. After all, a man whose thighs are no bigger around than my forearm doesn't take up much room.

The stench of such a place became something to dread on a hot spring afternoon. Vomit and urine and feces and foul breath and rotting bodies mingled their odors—the smell of 1,500 men in a single room half again or at most twice as long as one of our model barracks back home.

The camp used to be well guarded to keep the townspeople away, but they couldn't have lived in ignorance or innocence of what was going on here. Many of the prisoners worked in the nearby Weimar factories. They collapsed of hunger at their benches, and no one asked why. They died along the road on the long walk back to camp, and no one expressed surprise. . . .

Yank: The GI Story of the War (Duell, Sloan, and Pearce, 1947)

So Why
You Leave Me?

Still another Jewish immigration began after World War II when sur-
vivors of the Holocaust chose to resettle in America. By the time Hitler's
power was smashed, twenty-nine million people were dead. Among the
myriad slaughtered were the Jews—six million of them. How Jews think
of themselves today, and of the world they live in, has been shaped by
that knowledge. Jewish group behavior cannot be understood without
understanding the effects of the Holocaust.

Thousands of survivors have testified to the experience at the Holocaust.
One of them is Israel Green. He lived through the war and the death
camps and soon after resettled in New York and then in Chicago. His
testimony on the Holocaust and on his life in America speaks for many
like him.

Born in Poland, Israel Green was working as a diamond cutter in
Antwerp when the Nazi armies rolled into Belgium in 1940. Two
years later, the Nazis raided his home and sent his wife and two sons
to Auschwitz, where, he learned later, they died. Then he too was
sent.

I was taken to Auschwitz, too. They put us on a train. A
lot of people. So crowded. You know what I mean? We
couldn't stand, we couldn't sit. It was like sardines. It took
three days the journey. No water. No food. Did people
die? Oh, and how! Screaming and—I don't like to talk about
this. . . .

It was in the train car that people went to the toilet. It
was very dir—it was very.—it was no good.

We did not know we were going to a concentration camp.
You know what they say? They say that we going to see
the wives and children over there. They're going to unite

us with the wife and children. And that means I am so happy I cannot tell you. But who figured this?

When we got to the concentration camp there was the sign, *Arbeit Macht Frei.* Work Makes Free. And there was another sign that there was happiness here. Sure, it wasn't true. The whole thing what they did wasn't true.

So we come off the train now, herded off the train. *'Raus! 'Raus!* So they separate the people. Young mens, old mens separated. For me they took me to work. I carry cement on my back. Fifty kilo. One hundred fifty pounds. And breaking rocks with picks, with shovels.

Four in the morning we wake up in the concentration camp. Work all day until eight. In the night. They give for breakfast, for four people, a small bread. They cut the bread so that one had a bigger portion than the other. So they didn't care for you. For lunch and dinnertime a cold soup. Soup? Water! With a little potatoes. But you didn't have enough. Believe me. You could live, with this, four weeks. After four weeks, you have to be in the cemetery. I organized food. I didn't survive on their food, what they gave me.

So first of all, I had a lot of gold teeth in my mouth. I just fixed up my mouth in Belgium before they took me. There was gold in sixteen teeth. I took each one out myself. And I sold them to a German guard. He gave me money and I sold him teeth, because gold was expensive and valuable. I shake every night a tooth a little bit. Every night little bit because the gums are weak. Very weak. And not the first night, not the second night, little by little I took them out. I break them out. I have no teeth of my own left.

I only was looking to see what can I do to have food. That's all. The others were like me. Sometimes I would be beaten up.

156

And it was cold. We didn't have nothing to put on. We had only thin pajama.

At night we must stay outside. They count the people. If somebody run away, we must stand there all night. No food all night. The Germans say, "One for all and all for one." So that's why we have to suffer if somebody run away.

Some people escape. But many people they bring them back in the concentration camp to show us what's going to happen if we decide to run away. They took off their clothes from them and everybody must see this. Then they hang them. In the big yard. We must stay and see how they hang the people. And how they leave the people twenty-four hours. Saw sometimes twenty people, twenty-five people hang at a time. At dinnertime.

Why I was able to live? I had feeling in mine heart that I am going to survive. I keep hope in God. I had friends, they lost hope. They get sick, and I say, please, don't go hospital. From there you go right to the gas chamber. But they went to hospital and next thing, I see them naked on a truck. They go to be burned up.

I want to fight. I don't like to go suicide. There was nothing to live for, but I didn't want to be a murder over my own life. If I die, let somebody else kill me.

I do a lot of things to sabotage. And if they catch me, they kill me. But I didn't care! I steal bread from the kitchen. That's sabotage. I sneak potato to a friend. He sneaks one to me. That's sabotage. So many times I wish they catch me. I prayed to die. I was jealous because I see others die, just lie down and die. I couldn't die. I called myself a devil. But all the time I believe God will help us. Maybe a miracle will come to help us.

I meet a new wife. She was hiding in Switzerland during the war. Then we come to America. When I grew up in

Poland, I always hear of America. And many, many people went to America. Jewish people. But my family did not go. Not everybody was willing to go. My father was a Hebrew teacher. And he didn't have money for tickets for six children and a wife, who was sick. But my father used to say that, in America, the stones you walked on are *trayfeneh*. You know what trayfeneh means? They're not kosher. So the real religious people, they didn't like to go. Later I went to live in Belgium to make for myself a better life.

Well, I came to America and to East Flatbush. I work in a factory. But there are so many people. In Belgium I worked in mine house. So then we come to Chicago to be near the daughter. I got a job in a little factory. But I need more money. Somebody told me there is a market, so take this and this bus, change here this and this, and go over there. I had a friend. He gave me plastics to sell. I went to Maxwell Street, work on Sundays, on Saturdays, on holidays. I make a few dollars. I was happy.

I make enough from there that when my boy grow up, I send him to college. From this money that I make on Maxwell Street. I gave it for my son. He made me a big joy when he graduate from college.

I want to tell you. If you talk about freedom, I had more freedom in Belgium. You know why? Because I'm not afraid to walk over there the whole night. Nobody going to hurt me. That means freedom. If you have to be afraid for me, and I have to be afraid for you, is that freedom? If you are afraid to go out in the night whenever you want to go, is that freedom? Doesn't mean freedom to me.

My wife visited a friend one night. When she walks back, two guys beat her up. They want to take her purse. She didn't want to give it. She was taken to the hospital, and she was very, very sick. She, thank God, is home. Was last year.

When I lived in East Flatbush they kill away three butchers not far from me, three which they come from Europe. Young men.

That means, believe me, if I have to go to bed and sleep in the night, I have to look all over my doors. Oop, I didn't—forgot to lock something, to lock good. That means I live in fear. . . . A lot of times I got dreams, bad dreams from concentration camp. I want to scream from the sleep, but I can't. You know what I mean? When you sleep, your voice . . . doesn't go. You know?

Because old memories from SS. Very bad dreams. Crematoriums and . . . beating. Smoke from the crematorium. I used to work in that part of the camp. I used to see smoke and hear screams from children. Papa! Mama! They come from the trains. The people got out. *'Raus! 'Raus!* And the children, they was screaming. All the luggage. They separate the people.

I dream of eating like animals. We never had a spoon to eat. We never had a fork. The whole three years we never had a knife. Four people and one plate and the guard gave a piece of meat to me and one *shlep* to the other one. The one pulled it away and that one pulled it away and the other one pulled it away. I want to tell you. I prayed to God when I was over there that if I survive, I only want to have bread, as much as I need, and potatoes. And water. Nothing else.

So now I appreciate. I never throw away a piece of bread. When I go on the street, when I see bread, I pick them up and I put the bread somewhere, by a window—not to walk on bread.

Sure, sometime I complain. I don't like this food my wife make and I don't like that. That's the way it is. But I am happy with my life. I'm not looking to be rich. I say, "I got enough." My parents didn't have this, either. Why shouldn't I be happy? I got food. Or if I'm going to sit with people and talk like a human being. Is very nice. In the concentration camp, you talk this and this, they hang me up. Sabotage. Everything was sabotage. And I look at grass and trees now. So beautiful. I didn't see a tree for three years.

But with the dreams I have, and with this on my arm—it is hard to forget.

[He rolls up his sleeve. Engraved in black in his skin just above the left wrist is the number 66242.]

This is what I was known by. They never call you by name in the concentration camp. I see this now every morning when I wash.

But you can't live all the time with this memory. It would be very serious thing if you would dream every night about this. If you would talk every night about this. You don't have to forget completely, but you have to forget little by little.

My son, I start to tell him about the concentration camp, but he used to say, "Daddy, I'm American. Please don't tell me any of your stories from the old country."

As soon as he graduated college he told me he going to move to Boston. So I ask him, "Why you have to move to Boston? The same money you can make here."

He said, "Daddy, I got my own life. I like living over there and I think I can make more money." I feel very bad. Very, very bad. So he left. I don't care so much now. But my wife, she feels lonely. We have no relative, only the two children. But I tell her, "He got a right to live any way he want. It's his life." I did the same thing. When I left home from Poland to go to Belgium, my father asked me the same question, "So why you leave me?" And I didn't listen to him either.

Ira Berkow, *Maxwell Street* (New York: Doubleday, 1977)

Of Course
She's a Nice Girl

Soon after World War II the American middle class (including the Jews) expanded astonishingly in numbers. The children of the immigrants climbed up and up the economic ladder. They moved into better housing, in the cities and suburbs, and sent a large percentage of their children to college and to graduate school. As discrimination lessened, many more Jews turned from the world of business to the arts, sciences, and professions.

Most American Jews tried to integrate with American society, but without losing their ethnic identity. It was clear by now that the old melting-pot theory did not hold. As each immigrant group developed its own ethnic life, it contributed special qualities to the larger pattern of American life. Cultural pluralism this phenomenon was called. Still, the leaders of Jewish organizations began to worry about Jewish cultural survival in postwar America. They viewed assimilation and intermarriage as grave dangers. The birthrate among Jews showed a steady tendency to drop, and divorce rates among Jews began to rise.

Jews had always valued the close-knit family unit because they believed it had preserved them when other peoples had vanished. Intermarriage— the marriage of a Jew to a non-Jew—was once totally rejected by the Jewish community. But as Jews won more political and social equality following World War II, marriage outside the group became more common.

There was and still is, in many places, intense concern over interfaith dating. In the following narrative, Eli Evans describes this concern. Raised in Durham, North Carolina, Eli was the son of a department store owner, who in 1950 was elected mayor. With so few Jews in the South, Eli's parents sent him to Jewish summer camps to give him "maximum Jewish exposure." On the high school football squad, when he noticed in the shower room that he was the only circumcised player

Her name was Natalie, and together we were alone, she
the only Jewish girl and I the only Jewish boy in our class.
For years we smiled at each other in the halls, cautious
but affectionate, and slightly resentful that parents and the
Jewish community expected us to be romantically entan-
gled. We were friends, intimate and understanding, both
of us rebellious against the biblical force of history and
calling on each other for reassurance. When she went to
the junior-senior prom with Sykes Carter, my mother
blamed me; if I had not fallen from my duty, such a tragedy
would not have occurred. It was almost as embarrassing
when we did end up going to something with each other—
usually an important event like the senior class play, when
mothers really made an issue of it. Then, walking arm-
in-arm, we were both mortified because everybody knew
we didn't date ordinarily and that I was with her only because we were Jewish. Sometimes, gentile girls would say,
"You'll marry Natalie, won't you?" or make a point of reminding me that while they liked me a lot, if I didn't take
Natalie to a dance, she probably wouldn't be able to go
at all. Years later, when both of us gained perspective, she
told me that her mother expected her to be attractive enough
for me to take her out, and that she judged herself some
sort of failure if she didn't succeed. As we imagined it,
our mothers talked and plotted at Hadassah meetings, and
complained to each other of their miserable fate in such a
small town and hoped for the best.

But for two years my heart belonged at first secretly and
then openly to Liz Jordan, homecoming queen and acknowledged beauty of the class. She projected that graceful kind
of beauty that Southern girls have perfected through his-

tory, long brown hair framing big fluttering brown eyes, trusting and dreaming, with an easy smile that stirred the boys she graced with it—and she graced us all. We thought of her as aristocratic and "ree-fined," a proper girl to whom we attached all the essential Southern virtues—sweetness, softness, thoughtfulness, elegance, and modesty. Her mother was active in the Methodist church women's group, and she in the youth fellowship.

Liz was the classic Southern beauty; she walked with a long, confident gait, perhaps "flowed" is a better word, but didn't try athletics at lunch period, preferring to languish like a vision on the sidelines. She was serious in her studies but never openly smart, thus never a threat. She was popular even with girls because she never spoke a harsh word of others and worked hard at avoiding the terrible high-school charge of being "stuck-up." No one ever caught her primping; if there was any sexiness to her, it smoldered in her innocence, her lack of awareness of her power and unconcern for its impact; her most potent weapon was her unattainability, for few boys had the self-assurance to try.

Liz had what we called a "good reputation," and it was natural that everyone should vote her honors like homecoming queen and secretary of the student council, for she exemplified our aspirations for womankind. We had served as class officers together, and if I was selected president of the student council, not only would I have a good excuse for not going out for football the next year but Liz and I could work with each other over the summer, and I would probably be able to crown her homecoming queen at the game that fall. With lumbering Tom Lee, the big, bad defensive lineman and co-captain of the football team making the nomination speech for me at assembly, and a brisk campaign consisting of posters that said "Even Bugs Bunny Says Vote for Sonny" and "Your vote is a must for a guy you can trust," I won the right to kiss her cheek on that warm homecoming night, and exult in pictures of us together in the morning newspaper.

I walked her home from school each day and we would usually stop at the West Side Pharmacy for a Coke. After, at the corner a block from her house (and safely out of view of her mother), we would hesitantly brush good-bye. Finally, she invited me to be one of her escorts for the statewide debutante ball in Raleigh.

"You're not going and that's it. It's final. Final! Do you hear me?"

"But, Mom, it's only a dance."

We're doing it for your sake. Of course she's a nice girl— but that's just the point."

It was the first of several furious confrontations with my mother over not dating Jewish girls, which I usually resolved simply by not telling her. But this date required the rental of a white tie and tails, money for flowers, and the car for the weekend, and Mother won easily. Sadly I told Liz I had other plans. (It never helped to sneak out; at every movie I imagined there was somebody from the Jewish community to spy on me and report back.)

Eli N. Evans, *The Provincials: A Personal History of Jews in the South* (New York: Atheneum, 1973)

To Make Things Grow

On the birth of the independent state of Israel in 1948, the new country flung wide its doors to immigrants. Settlers came from all over the world. Among them were thousands of American Jews. Even before the proclamation of independence, some Americans joined the Jewish forces in the three-way struggle for Palestine waged among the Jews, Arabs, and

British. That war (and those that followed) tapped deep Jewish feelings. American Jews felt Israel's survival also meant their survival. It was not a question of allegiance to the United States, but of solidarity with the new Jewish state.

Among those ready to give Israel their support, and their lives, was Daniel Spicehandler. Born in New York in 1923, he joined the Haganah and fought during the siege of Jerusalem. For a time he worked on a kibbutz, one of the cooperative settlements (they were both agricultural and industrial) that contributed to Israel's development far beyond their numbers. Here he tells what drew a young American to so different a life.

I got up one morning a little late. I ran down to the dining hall to see where I was scheduled to work. I looked down the work sheet and saw my name under orchards. I was to report to Moshe, the head orchard man. I had heard that he was one of the *vatikim,* founders, of this *kibbutz,* one of the original twelve who settled here years back. Today Ginegar had over four hundred occupants. I thought that it would be interesting to work with this old pioneer, a *chalutz,* a type that had once been the hero of modern Palestine. He was a short, fat man with graying hair at the temples. His eyes were watery blue and he immediately reminded me of my father. His gray patched pants were caked with mud. He was standing near a large faucet, watching the irrigation of the surrounding apple trees.

"Shalom, I'm Donny," I said.

"Oh Yes. *Tov,* good, you shall work with me. We shall direct the waters around the trees." He spoke Hebrew as a Sabra, but with a slightly musical intonation he had never lost from his former Yiddish-speaking days. I walked with a hoe, moving the mud, banking it into little dams, not allowing the waters around the trees to overflow.

"Did you ever farm in America?" he asked.

"No, I was a student," I answered. He smiled.

"All Jews are students or shop owners. I was a student once. Now I am a farmer." He said it simply, with so much dignity. I looked up at him. His face was creased with lines, his eyes were tired. He was all tanned and looked like a teacher who was forced into hard physical labor which didn't agree with him.

"Tell me," he asked, "are there many Jews in America who wish to come here?"

"No, not many, especially not to the *kibbutzim.*" I patted a bank of mud with the side of my shoe. He smiled and a line cracked around his flabby cheeks.

"You know, son, the *kibbutz* movement will never cater to the many. We shall always be small and compact. It's much too hard a life for the average person to see the beauty of it." I bent down and banked some more mud with my hand. He continued.

"Take this orchard. I raised it. I know its childhood, its love, its marriages. I educated it to grow, to produce healthy fruit, healthy children. They know me, these trees. I am their God, their protector." I stopped working and looked about me. The orchard sloped up a hill. On two sides lay the *kibbutz,* on the other two sides were barren rocky hills. Fifteen years ago this orchard had been in wedlock to those arid hills.

"I like you Americans," said Moshe. He stopped working and leaned on his hoe. His shoes were rimmed with a flat layer of mud and they looked like snowshoes. "You came here as we did. Free, from nice comfortable homes, not forced by circumstances like those coming today from Europe. We need people who are of healthy mind and body for the *kibbutzim.* We need youths like yourself. It is asking too much of the European Jews of today to find themselves in this strange society of ours. But you, you Americans, can and will find yourselves here."

166

"It's a very hard life," I said. "I was raised in a city, the largest city, and the truth of the matter is that I miss it."

"So do I. I miss the city. The stores, the cafés, the theaters, bookstores. But you never miss them and rarely go to them when you do live in the city. You live and live, then you die and only your children remember you. What about society, life? I believe we are given the greatest privilege when we are born. Life is loaned to us and we must repay this debt, pay society for this privilege. Mere existing is 'sponging' off society. My God is this privilege, this gift of birth. I worship it and pay my tithe to it, and this I do through my *kibbutz.*"

The sun began to beat down on my head. I dipped my hands into the muddy waters and splashed them on my face. It felt good.

"You Americans believe in God," continued Moshe. "Your God is made into a parasite by you. He sits and does nothing and you worship Him, be it in a Jewish way or a Christian way. My God is a creator, a worker who needs to be aided in the tremendous job He has. I worship Him by my will to create, to make things grow."

Moshe, a *chalutz,* a philosopher, a farmer. Here was the type of man I had read about in Zionist literature, a character I had met in many modern Hebrew novels. He was the peasant philosopher, a Tolstoy perhaps. I envied him.

Daniel Spicehandler, *Let My Right Hand Wither* (Boston: Beechhurst, 1950)

A Note on Sources

The voices heard in this book originally were recorded in many different places. The reader or student interested in finding more Jewish American documents has many sources to go to. A number of anthologists have published volumes of documents, and more are sure to appear.

Works intended primarily for scholars include Jacob R. Marcus's two-volume *EARLY AMERICAN JEWRY, 1649–1794,* (Jewish Publication Society, 1951); the same editor's three-volume *MEMOIRS OF AMERICAN JEWS, 1775–1865,* (KTAV, 1974); his *THE AMERICAN JEWISH WOMAN, 1654–1980* (KTAV, 1981); and Morris U. Schappes's *A DOCUMENTARY HISTORY OF THE JEWS IN THE UNITED STATES, 1654–1875* (Schocken, 1971).

For the general reader there are collections that focus on a particular period, place, or theme or draw from a single periodical. Examples are Milton Hindus's, *THE OLD EAST SIDE* (Jewish Publication Society, 1971); Azriel Eisenberg, *THE GOLDEN LAND* (Yoseloff, 1964); Isaac Metzker's, *A BINTEL BRIEF* (Ballantine, 1972).

More recently, historians have used the tape recorder to gather and document oral histories, their own and the narratives of others. For perspective on survivors of the Holocaust living in America there is Dorothy Rabinowitz's *NEW LIVES* (Knopf, 1976). For the experience of the Great Depression there is Ann Banks's *FIRST PERSON AMERICA* (Knopf, 1980), or Studs Terkel's *HARD TIMES* (Pantheon, 1970), both of which contain interviews with Jews. For a study of Jews in old age living in a California community there is Barbara Myerhoff's, *NUMBER OUR DAYS* (Simon & Schuster), 1978.

Some writers have focused on the lives of Jewish women: Charlotte Baum, Paula Hyman, and Sonya Michel, *THE JEW-*

ISH WOMAN IN AMERICA (New American Library, 1975), and Sidelle Kramer and Jenny Masur, *JEWISH GRANDMOTHERS* (Beacon, 1976). One writer has confined his docu nentation .of Jewish experience to a single city—Chicago: Ira Berkow, *MAXWELL STREET* (Doubleday, 1977). For material on the arrival of east European Jews in the port of New York, there are such works as Allan Schoener's *PORTAL TO AMERICA* (Holt, 1967).

Beyond these, and in such quantity as to forbid listing here, there are the autobiographies, memoirs, diaries, letters of Jewish Americans. The reader will note my use of them.

From time to time the historical journals, both Jewish and general, print documents bearing on Jewish life. And of course the archives and research libraries in the field of Jewish studies continually gather documents, which are accessible to the student. For a list of the major institutions, apply to the Council of Archives and Research Libraries in Jewish Studies, Suite 1512, 122 East 42nd Street, New York, N.Y. 10036.

Index

MILTON MELTZER, historian and biographer, has written over fifty books reflecting his deep interest in the struggle for freedom and justice. Several of his books on aspects of Jewish history were National Book Award nominees: *Never to Forget: The Jews of the Holocaust*; *World of Our Fathers: The Jews of Eastern Europe*; and *Remember the Days: A Short History of Jewish America*. His books on ethnic and black history include *The Chinese Americans*; *The Hispanic Americans*; *In Their Own Words: A History of the American Negro*; and *All Times, All Peoples: A World History of Slavery*.

Born in Worcester, Massachusetts, and educated at Columbia University, Mr. Meltzer lives in New York City, is married, and has two daughters.

Format by Megan Lloyd
Set in 11 pt. Video Comp Compano
Composed by Kingsport Press
Printed and bound by Halliday Lithograph Corporation
Thomas Y. Crowell